THE
NEW
DEBTORS'
PRISON

Why All Americans Are in Danger
Of Losing Their Freedom

BY CHRISTOPHER MASELLI
WITH PAUL LONARDO

Skyhorse Publishing

Skyhorse Publishing books may be purchased in bulk at special discounts for sales promotion, corporate gifts, fund-raising, or educational purposes. Special editions can also be created to specifications. For details, contact the Special Sales Department, Skyhorse Publishing, 307 West 36th Street, 11th Floor, New York, NY 10018 or info@skyhorsepublishing.com.

Skyhorse Publishing® is an imprint of Skyhorse Publishing, Inc.®, a Delaware corporation.

Visit our website at www.skyhorsepublishing.com.

10 9 8 7 6 5 4 3 2 1

Library of Congress Cataloging-in-Publication Data is available on file.

Cover design by Rain Saukas

Print ISBN: 978-1-51073-325-1
Ebook ISBN: 978-1-51073-326-8

Printed in the United States of America

CONTENTS

INTRODUCTION

BY PAUL LONARDO

CHRISTOPHER MASELLI, A father, husband, lawyer, and an up-and-coming state senator, was approached one day in 2008 by the Federal Bureau of Investigation to assist them in building criminal cases against friends and colleagues in a failing and floundering federal corruption probe into Rhode Island politics. However, when he refused to sell out his friends and cooperate with the Federal Government, Chris was indicted by a Federal Grand Jury in 2010 and served twenty-seven months in Federal Prison, not for political corruption, but for trumped-up charges of lying on personal mortgage applications. After his release, Chris emerged to try to get his life back in order, but it was not easy. In a state like Rhode Island, known as much for its corrupt politicians as anything else, where everybody knows everybody, Chris was presumed guilty of acts of misconduct and crimes that he did not commit. With his license to practice law suspended, and his reputation sullied, his personal and family life turned upside down, he had to start over again.

Chris's passion for criminal justice and prison reform comes from his experience as a lawyer, policy maker, former inmate, and head of the prison education department. When the bubble burst on the prosperity of the real estate bubble of the early 2000s, Chris watched consumers and mid-level banking and real estate professionals come under criminal scrutiny. While the CEOs of our nation's financial institutions have paid billions of dollars in fines and settlements to avoid prosecution because they can afford to, the middle-class routinely gets shafted. As a group, they are helpless, with no bail out for them; and without financial resources, prison is what awaits hardworking Americans who get caught in desperate financial straits.

Today, thanks to second chances, Chris is once again a practicing criminal and civil attorney, but many are unable to rebound after being incarcerated in what amounts to modern debtors' prisons.

THE
NEW DEBTORS' PRISON

1

A BRIEF HISTORY
OF DEBTORS' PRISONS

BY MOST ACCOUNTS, the birthplace of the debtors' prison was Victorian England, during the period of Queen Victoria's reign, from 1837 until her death in 1901. While this will be proven not to be wholly accurate, there is sound reason why this era is seen as the golden age, if you will, of debtors' prisons. Law and order was a major issue at that time. With the expansion and growth of cities throughout England following the Industrial Revolution, Victorians were worried about the rising crime rate, seeing offenses go up from about 5,000 per year in 1800 to about 20,000 per year in 1840.[1] They were firm believers in punishment for criminals.

Until the late 18th century in England, it was unusual to imprison guilty people for long terms. Hanging and transportation were the main punishments for serious offenses. "Transportation" was the practice of sending convicted criminals, or other persons regarded as undesirable, to a penal colony. This form of banishment, or forced exile, has been used as a punishment since at least Ancient Roman times. It removed the offender from society, possibly permanently, but was seen as a more merciful punishment than execution. Instead of being hanged, Britain transported its criminals to Australia to serve their prison sentences. Over the years, about 160,000 people were sent to penal colonies in Australia, which included women and children, sometimes as young as nine years old. During the 18th century, the British government also sent prisoners to penal colonies in America, usually for seven years or sometimes for life. This practice ceased when the American War of Independence broke out in 1775.[2]

Prisons served as temporary lockups and places where the accused were kept before their trial. However, by the Victorian era, prison became an acceptable form of punishment for a wide variety of offenses, and it was also seen as a means to prevent crime. As towns grew and crime levels increased, people became more and more concerned about how to keep criminals under control. But there was also public unease at the number of hangings. By the 1830s, many areas in Australia were refusing to be the "dumping-ground" for Britain's criminals. The answer was to reform the police and to build more prisons: ninety prisons were built or added to between 1842 and 1877—a massive building program, costing millions of pounds.[3]

A WALK ON THE WILDE SIDE

By the middle of the Victorian period, there were two distinct prison systems in England. There were the county and shire *gaols* (*gaol* is a British term for jail), administered by Justices of the Peace. These ranged from small lockups to large "County Gaols" or "Houses of Correction." The second system was the "Convict Gaols" run by the central government in London. Gradually, the use of convict gaols came to include holding prisoners as part of the process of transportation to other countries. Newgate was the main prison in this system. There were also three convict prisons at Millbank, Pentonville, and Brixton. Decommissioned naval vessels, called "hulks," were used to house prisoners and became part of the convict gaol system. Other convict gaols were situated at ports. The hulks were old sailing ships at south coast harbors or on the Thames at Woolwich. Originally used as holding prisons, the hulks were used more and more to house ordinary prisoners at the end of the French Wars due to the shortage of prisons. At one point, over two-thirds of all prisoners were on the hulks. Conditions in the hulks were horrible. During outbreaks of disease such as cholera, large numbers of prisoners died because of the unsanitary conditions on board and because all-purpose water came from the polluted Thames. Prisoners were chained to their bunks at night to prevent them from slipping ashore. During the day, most of them worked ashore, usually on hard labor. The last of the hulks burned down in 1857, but their use had lessened in the ten years before then.[4]

The Victorians had a clear idea about the function of prisons. They were intended to be unpleasant places to deter people from committing crimes. Prisoners were forced to do hard, boring work for no real purpose. Walking a treadwheel and picking oakum (separating the scraps in fibers of old Navy ropes) for many hours were the most common forms of hard labor.[5]

In 1895, Irish playwright, poet, and novelist Oscar Wilde was sentenced to two years' hard labor. While incarcerated, he was required to declare bankruptcy, by which he essentially lost all his possessions including his books and manuscripts. Like the other prisoners, he was allowed to read only the Bible and *The Pilgrim's Progress*. They could not speak to one another, and outside of their solitary cells, the inmates were required to wear a cap with a sort of thick veil so as not be recognized. Wilde finished out his sentence at the prison at Reading and upon his release wrote *The Ballad of Reading Gaol*, a response to the agony he experienced in prison and providing an interesting insight into what prison life was like for an upper-class male:

> *Like two doomed ships that pass in storm*
> *We had crossed each other's way:*
> *But we made no sign, we said no word,*
> *We had no word to say;*
> *For we did not meet in the holy night,*
> *But in the shameful day.*

A prison wall was round us both,
Two outcast men were we:
The world had thrust us from its heart,
And God from out His care:
And the iron gin that waits for Sin
Had caught us in its snare.

In Debtors' Yard the stones are hard,
And the dripping wall is high,
So it was there he took the air
Beneath the leaden sky,
And by each side a Warder walked
For fear the man might die.[6]

These were hard, unruly places, where prisoners had to provide their own food and had little access to fresh water. Each prison was run by the *gaoler* (jailer) in his own way. He made up the rules. A prisoner had to pay the gaoler for every service, even for putting them in irons as a punishment. Those who had no money were forced to beg from local people passing the prison.[7] There was no protection against other prisoners. Those who caused the most trouble were shackled in irons or whipped. Prisoners could obtain early release if they behaved well, as long as they were not in debt. If you could pay, you could buy extra privileges, such as private rooms, better food, more visitors, keeping pets, letters going in and out, and books to read. If you could not, the basic fare was grim. You even had to pay the gaoler to be let out when your sentence was finished.

Prisons at this time were often in old buildings, even castles, and as such tended to be damp, cold, unsanitary, and overcrowded. The conditions were deplorable. They were filthy and infested with rats, lice, and fleas. It is said that these places were so squalid that around 25 percent of inmates died due to disease, neglect, and starvation.[8] All kinds of prisoners were mixed in together: men, women, and children; the insane; violent criminals and petty criminals; people awaiting trial; and debtors.

THE WALKING DEBT

Debtors were by far the largest element in the 18th-century prison population, with more than half the prisoners in England imprisoned for debt, though most were often innocent tradespeople who had fallen on hard times. A person could be sent to debtors' prison in Victorian England for owing the slightest amounts of money. Approximately 10,000 people were imprisoned for debt each year during the nineteenth century.[9]

In Victorian England, the concepts of credit and debt were closely linked to that of a person's character. Credit was not only based on a person's assets and income, but it also determined their social status within the community. Going into debt was seen as a moral failure, not merely an economic circumstance, and it was punished accordingly. As such, this system typically favored the upper classes. It was more difficult for the working classes to obtain credit, and if they went into debt, the penalties they incurred were more severe than those issued to the upper classes. County Court judges, who presided over debt and bankruptcy cases, often issued rulings based on the belief that the working classes defaulted on their debts deliberately. In contrast, the upper classes were seen as having an honest desire to repay their debt and were given more lenient treatment. Declaring bankruptcy allowed a debtor to avoid prison, but this was not an option available to everyone. Until 1861, it was limited to the merchant class. Furthermore, the cost of filing for bankruptcy was ten pounds,[10] which represented 10–20 percent of the average annual income for the common worker in the mid-1860s.[11]

What is referred to as a debtors' prison is any jail or detention facility that incarcerates people for their inability, refusal, or failure to pay a debt. They are people whose creditors took legal action against them and had them thrown in prison until the debt was paid. The fate of the debtors lay with the creditors, who determined what happened to the debtors. Some creditors were known to torture their debtors for pleasure.

Debtors' prisons were also known as *workhouses*, or *poorhouses*, where the prisoners would make potato sacks, baskets, and other mass-produced items.[12] Debtors' prisons, which could be small jailhouses resembling small houses or sheds, were quite common in Western Europe through the mid-nineteenth century.

Because men were held responsible for households' financial matters, nearly all imprisoned debtors were male.[13] With the father imprisoned, the family business often suffered while the mother and children fell into poverty. Debtors in prison who were unable to pay the debt often remained there for many years, and since indefinite incarceration was the mode of punishment, if a debtor had a family, his spouse and children might well accompany him in prison, though family members were free to come and go according to their wishes. Entire communities sprang up inside the debtors' prisons, with children being born and raised there. Some debt prisoners were released to become serfs or indentured servants (debt bondage) until they paid off their debt in labor.

Debtors' prisons did allow their inmates some degree of freedoms, yet it required purchases, as incongruous as that sounds, considering these men were behind bars because they did not have enough money to pay what they already owed. Some were even allowed to live a short distance outside the prison, a practice known as the "Liberty of the Rules."[14]

Debtors' prisons were privately run institutions that functioned like an extortion racket, with whole economies created around their inhabitants. In addition to prison keepers charging residents for food and board, bailiffs charged for food and clothing, attorneys charged legal fees in fruitless efforts to get the debtors out, and creditors, often tradesmen, increased the debt simply because the debtor was in prison. Debts could accumulate to the point where there was no realistic prospect of release.[15]

If the prison did supply food to its nonpaying inmates, charitable donations from the local parish paid for it. And for those who were genuinely destitute, conditions were much more intolerable. Inmates would resort to begging for coins from passers-by through the bars on their windows, and some starved to death.

The prison had separate areas for its two classes of prisoners: the master's side and the commoner side. On the master's side, room rents were ten shillings a week for a room with two beds, shared with up to three other prisoners. There was a bar; a chandler's shop, which sold candles, soap, and a little food; a coffee shop; a steakhouse; a tailor; and a barber. These were the prisoners who would be allowed out during the day, which gave them a chance to earn money for their creditors. Prisoners from the master's side could also hire prisoners from the common side to act as their servants—one way that the commoner prisoners would make money. On the commoner side, everyone was crammed into one of nine small rooms with dozens of others, possibly for years for the most modest of debts, which increased as unpaid prison fees accumulated. The poorest faced starvation and were dressed in rags, unkempt and unshaven. If they crossed the jailers, they would be tortured with skullcaps and thumbscrews.[16]

While other European countries had legislation limiting imprisonment for debt to one year, debtors in England were kept behind bars until their creditors were satisfied, however long that took. When the Fleet Prison closed in 1842, some debtors were found to have been there for thirty years.[17]

It was a desperate situation for many, as the following letter written by a debtor in King's Bench Prison in Southwark clearly testifies. On July 20, 1827, M. Eurius Beaubrier addressed Henry Clarke:

More than three months have elapsed since first I entered these walls and God knows what I have been my suffering during that time. I have settled two of the actions against me, and I can obtain my discharge on my last for about five pounds. I shall trespass on your friendship once more and for the last time and shall beg of you to lend me the amount which I shall faithfully repay with what you had the kindness to advance me already. I shall be indebted to you for my liberty, which I have learned to appreciate after so long a confinement.

I hope that the country air has been beneficial to you and that you are recovered from your late illness. Mrs. Beaubrier writes to say that they have received letters from Sir William Congreve and that he finds himself much better.

I remain, Dear sir, Your ever grateful,
M. Eurius Beaubrier.[18]

Fleet Prison was one of only a few institutions that catered solely to debtors, so many debtors were sent to prisons that housed a mix of petty and vicious criminals, though debtors were kept in separate wings. Newgate, for instance, was London's main prison. It was ancient, complete with a dungeon, and for much of the 19th century, it was where inmates awaiting to be executed were held. The gallows were outside the prison walls, and the condemned were executed before large, clamoring crowds.

Apart from Newgate and the Fleet, other London prisons that housed debtors included Coldbath Fields Prison, King's Bench Prison, and Marshalsea, which became arguably the most notorious Victorian-era prison. Marshalsea, built in the late 14th century, was located south of the River Thames in what is today London. It housed a variety of prisoners over the centuries, including men accused of crimes at sea and political figures charged with sedition, but it became known, in particular, for its incarceration of the poorest of London's debtors.[19] The Marshalsea was far from occupied by the dregs of society, with many of the imprisoned debtors coming from the more "respectable" sections of society, often as the result of having spent more than they could afford just to keep up appearances. Besides Oscar Wilde, a number of other well-known writers served time as inmates in debtors' prisons, including *Robinson Crusoe* and *Moll Flanders* author Daniel Defoe and, in Spain in the late 16th century, Cervantes, who began writing *Don Quixote* while in a debtors' prison. The experiences these writers had not only affected them on a personal level, but they also inspired them to share their stories in their works, which allowed others to see the human suffering by putting a face on the men, women, and children who were locked up in prisons throughout Britain.

In *Moll Flanders*, Daniel Defoe described the horrific conditions inside the walls of Newgate this way:

> *I looked around upon all the horrors of that dismal place. I looked on myself as lost, and that I had nothing to think of but going out of the world, and that with the utmost infamy: the hellish noise, the roaring, swearing, and clamor, the stench and nastiness, and all the dreadful crowd of afflicting things that I saw there, joined together to make the place seem an emblem of hell itself, and a kind of an entrance into it.*[20]

Famed British writer and social critic Charles Dickens was just twelve years old when he was forced to work at a shoe polish factory to help support his family after his father was sent to the Marshalsea in 1824 because he owed a local baker £40. It was a defining life experience from which Dickens would later draw inspiration in many of his literary works. In his pen-portrait of a visit to Newgate prison, the ancient and notorious jail on the edge of the City of London, Charles Dickens wrote,

> *The girl belonged to a class—unhappily but too extensive—the very existence of which should make men's hearts bleed. Barely past her childhood, it required but a glance to discover that she was one of those children, born and bred in neglect and vice, who have never known what childhood is. . . . Talk to THEM of parental solicitude, the happy days of childhood,*

and the merry games of infancy! Tell them of hunger and the streets, beg-
gary and stripes, the gin-shop, the station-house, and the pawnbroker's, and
they will understand you.[21]

DEBT AND TAXES

So the obvious question then is why was debt was so prevalent in 19-century England? In order to understand debt in Victorian-era England, you have to keep in mind that this was a time of unprecedented population explosion. One of the reasons for this was that there were no catastrophic epidemics or famines. The devastating epidemics like smallpox, typhoid, and cholera gradually disappeared. The high birth rates resulting from dropping infant mortality, coupled with fewer deaths as people's overall health improved, greatly increased Britain's population. The progress and advances in medical science were good for society, but it had a detrimental impact on the economy. Despite the many jobs that the Industrial Revolution brought to the city, unemployment was high. There were several reasons for this, including automation that put jobs such as hand weavers out of business. With longer life spans, lower infant mortality rates, and improved health, there were simply more people than there were jobs. The resulting overabundance of workers also enabled factory owners to keep wages low, leaving many people either unemployed or underemployed. This change in the economic landscape caused families to go into debt. Additionally, England was in debt from the Napoleonic wars. The cost of the wars was nearly £1 billion, and by the end of the conflict in 1815, the British national debt soared to £679 million. Top all this off with deflation of the pound, and you have a volatile combination.[22]

How was all of this going to be paid? The taxpayer, of course.

Determining the exact the cost of living in Victorian England is complicated for several reasons. The first is that the Victorian period lasted a good long time, during which the UK went from being a largely rural, lightly industrialized country to a heavily industrialized urban nation. Also, the extended period of growth was followed by slumps at the end of the nineteenth century. The relationship between income and expenditure in Victorian England is difficult to equate with present-day figures because of the changes in the inherent value of goods. A worker in 1870 might make 150 percent of what a worker just twenty years before made, but because different prices had increased at different rates, the actual buying power of the wages increased only moderately. At the end of the century, prices fell considerably, more rapidly than wages, so that despite a lower wage, the workers' buying power increased. In the Victorian era, wages could vary dramatically from employer to employer in the same industry. On the low end of the spectrum, manufacturing workers in 1880 earned just $8 a month, compared to the more than $166 a month that the top-paying manufacturing firms paid their employees during the same period. Rising wage disparity in the 19th century was attributed, in part, to the growing numbers of workers who were finding employment in very large establishments, which generally paid far less than their smaller counterparts.[23]

However, it was more than just the economy that was changing, affecting the population of debtors' prisons—Victorian attitudes toward these institutions changed, as well.

By the 1860s, Victorians were largely of the opinion that most criminals were habitual and nothing would change them, and they just had to be scared enough by imprisonment to never offend again. People wanted prison reform for different reasons. Christian reformers felt that prisoners were God's creatures and deserved to be treated decently. Rational reformers believed that the purpose of prison was to punish and reform, not to kill prisoners with disease or teach them how to be better criminals.

During the first part of 18th century, when the British government transported prisoners to the colony of Georgia in America, it was done in the name of prison reform. James Oglethorpe, a British soldier, Member of

Parliament, and humanitarian, worked tirelessly to reform Britain's prison system after seeing the horrible conditions and abusive behavior prisoners endured. As a result of his advocacy, Parliament released many debtors from prison early; but with no means of support, and deposited into big cities, particularly London, they often became impoverished or resorted to criminal activity. Unable to eradicate or prevent the extreme number of poor people living in England, who were ultimately jailed for small offenses, including unpaid debts, Oglethorpe petitioned to establish a colony in Georgia to transform the prisoners into hardworking people with a trade: farmers, merchants, or artisans. In 1733, after months of travel, Oglethorpe and 114 men, women, and children arrived in Georgia and settled along the Savannah River. Oglethorpe's plan was a brilliant one. However, King George II had only given Oglethorpe the charter to advance England's economic circumstances as well as to serve as a buffer to the Spanish military in Florida. Because Oglethorpe had to focus all of his attention, energy, and resources on the Spanish in the south, his dream of an ideal agrarian society of reformed debtors had to be stalled and, in the end, never fulfilled.[24]

The actual transition concerning the overhaul of debtors' prisons in England was evident as far back as 1831 and later, when it was decreed that people who owed small amounts of money would be subjected to lenient treatment, unlike those who were repeat offenders or those with massive debts to settle. The small debtors were expected to be detained in their own cells away from those with huge debts or the general criminal or civilian prisoners. These regulations marked the beginning of a significant period in which debtors would be given better considerations, moving away from the darker days of European and English debtors' prisons.

The Victorian Age also brought reforms to debt relief. In 1844, the Insolvency Act abolished imprisonment for debts under £20, allowed private persons to become bankrupt, and lowered the financial limit to £50. The 1861 Bankruptcy Act abolished the Court for the Relief of Insolvent Debtors. Those imprisoned for debt could apply to the court to be released (unless they were in trade or guilty of fraudulent or other dishonest behavior) by reaching an agreement with their creditors that ensured a fair distribution of their present and future assets and transferred its jurisdiction to the Bankruptcy Court. All of which resulted in a dramatic fall in the number of debtors in prison.[25]

In 1868, another Act was introduced that provided even greater specifics regarding who could be considered a debtor. In this Act, debtors were people who had the means to pay their creditors but had willingly and knowingly refused to do so. The law treated them as those who were in contempt of court and could be sent to debtors' prisons. A year later, the government abolished all debtors' prisons in England. The Debtors Act of 1869 was an Act of the Parliament of the United Kingdom of Great Britain and Ireland that aimed at reforming the powers of courts to detain debtors.[26] While setting a new stage for the treatment of debtors, those with the capability to pay their creditors who refused to do so willingly could still be jailed, as could those who defaulted on payments to the court. The Act did not so much abolish the jailing of people for failing to pay their debts as significantly reduce the ability of the courts to detain those in debt.

Further reform followed through the Bankruptcy Act of 1883. These Acts initially reduced the amount of debtors sentenced to prison, but by the early twentieth century, the annual amount had risen to 11,427, an increase of nearly 2,000 from 1869.[27] Much of the Act has been repealed, but some provisions, such as the section relating to the judgment summons procedure, have survived.

THE NEW DEBTORS' PRISONS IN ENGLAND

Recently, there have been cases that have been taken up in the Centre for Criminal Appeals based in London, where people get jailed for failing to pay council tax debts and fines. The draconian laws that were used to jail citizens for failing to settle their debts have just come up in new forms.

According to the report by the National Association of Probation Officers 2015 report, the number of people incarcerated for failing to pay their debts has increased like never before. The belief that debtors' prisons ended a long time ago is a big fallacy; they are still in operation in Britain, with more and more people being jailed for not settling debts. These institutions have had, and continue to have, a dire impact on the lives of all citizens, not just those who have been jailed.

Furthermore, the debtors' prisons have resulted in many poor citizens being jailed with no avenue for salvation. The poor have filled most of the prisons because of failing to pay council taxes and fines while the affluent maneuver their ways with a lot of ease. All stakeholders should work together to ensure the rights of the poor are protected and that the authorities are checked against misusing their powers to collect illegal fees and fines and to stop illegal arrests and harassment of those who are unable to settle debts.

EARLY AMERICAN HISTORY OF DEBTORS' PRISONS

The founders of a new colony, whatever Utopia of human virtue they might originally project, have invariably regarded it among their earliest practical necessities to allot a portion of the virgin soil as a cemetery, and another portion as the site of a prison.[28]

Nathaniel Hawthorne begins *The Scarlet Letter* with a reflection about the need for cemeteries and prisons, suggesting that whatever Utopia is established, there always will be death, and there always will be crime, that this is just part of humans living in a community. This theory isn't just applicable to Puritan New England, but to any new colony at any time in history.

As settlers arrived in their newfound land, prisons were, indeed, some of the first buildings erected. Unlike today, these early prisons in America were not places where criminals were housed for long periods of time. In fact, most punishments were dealt with in terms of fines, public shame, physical chastisement, and death. Many people held in jail were awaiting trial and received their punishment immediately once a verdict was rendered. The only exceptions usually involved the offense of debt, which commonly brought periods of long-term incarceration.

The first American settlement was established in 1607 at Jamestown, Virginia. Many of the 104 men and boys who arrived by ships were under indenture contracts and were in servitude to the Virginia Company, which had the charter from the King of England to establish the first English settlement in North America. While these indenture contracts were entered into freely and voluntarily, many of the first colonists were imprisoned debtors in England, and the contracts were entered forcibly. So, to some degree, the start of the first colony in America was established on the backs of inmates of English debtors' prisons. Those debtors came in hopes of escaping their debt, but to do this, they had to become indebted to the Virginia Company.[29]

As in England, common law allowed creditors to imprison debtors as an avenue of collection. There was the *writ of capias ad respondendum,* or in simple terms an arrest warrant for a debtor when a lawsuit commenced. The *writ of capias ad satisfaciendum* was a warrant upon the body of a debtor once a creditor obtained a judgment. The colonies and the states, post-Revolutionary War, kept remains of these English procedures in place. There are estimations that as many as two out of every three Europeans who immigrated to America in the 17th and 18th centuries were in debt as soon as they arrived in the New World. To many, the only option available to cross the Atlantic was by entering into indentured servitude to pay their price of travel.

WORKING-CLASS DEBT

The attack on the working class started early on in American history. In 1638, the Massachusetts Bay Colony ruled that anyone delinquent on their taxes could be jailed. However, if a court determined that the taxpayer was too poor to pay his overdue taxes, that person was set free, leaving only the struggling working-class people to spend their time in prison for outstanding taxes. As early as a year later, debtors of private debt were being jailed, too. Then in 1641, Massachusetts courts ruled that any person owing money to private creditors may be imprisoned until the debt was paid off.[30] These rulings revolutionized not only the public sphere, but also the private sector. A lot of individuals found their ways into prisons due to their inability to pay debts, with few managing to come out. Debtors' prisons at this time created quite the paradox. Inmates of debtors' prisons in the early American colonies, just as the ones across the ocean in England, were forced to pay the cost of their incarceration and repay their debts, even though they were given no viable means or opportunity to pay off the debt. If a debtor did obtain a release, it was due to a family member or outside sources paying their way to freedom.

The 17th century also became a period that began to see some transformations, at least in thought, about debtors' prisons, even as the incarceration institutions for those who couldn't settle their debts or pay taxes increased further. A Maryland statute, passed in 1639, stated that any insolvent debtor would have to assign his property to the creditor in proportion to the debts he owes. Debtors had the option of insolvency, where they would work for their creditors in declining sequence until the debts were settled in full. In 1682, the Pennsylvania authorities followed Massachusetts' lead and came up with a law to collect debts from insolvent debtors. The law stated that anyone arrested for failing to pay a debt would be kept in prison. The creditors in those cases could permit a debtor to pay off the debt through servitude and work toward their release.

Regarding the plights of debtors in the United States, the trend of incarceration and suffering continued to grow exponentially. It was apparent that further reforms were crucial, prompting a sequence of changes to some of the laws. Actual reform began in 1729, when Pennsylvania officially came up with debt servitude requiring any debtor to serve his creditor until fully settling the debt. In circumstances where the debtor was released from prison, the debt was still in place and could be collected should the debtor obtain any property in the future. More crucial reforms came with the passing of the Act for the Relief and Release of Poor Prisoners for Debt and Damages in Massachusetts. The Act allowed for the release of debt prisoners in exchange for taking an oath after serving one month. If a prisoner were to swear that he was unable to settle his debts and that he had not transferred or hidden his wealth to defraud his creditors, he could be released based on the Act.[31]

In 1732, the English crown chartered its last American colony, Georgia, when King George II appointed James Edward Oglethorpe, a trustee who later led the first colonists to the settlement in Savannah. As mentioned earlier, for Oglethorpe, an English political activist who chaired a parliamentarian committee on British prison reform, things did not turn out as planned, and none of the first settlers were actually debtors. Slavery was banned, but that too changed by 1750, when African slaves were imported into Georgia.[32]

As the colonies became more commercialized and industrialized, debts became more rampant. The interchange of goods and commodities between England and the colonies was substantial, and so was debt prior to the American Revolution, causing creditors to be more active in using the writs influenced by English law. The threat of imprisonment for failing to pay a debt was strong and influential. Therefore, debtors handed over property voluntarily to pay bills and stay out of prison. In that sense, debtors' prisons actually worked *for creditors*, with the dreadful side effects of long-term imprisonment and life sentences all but ignored.

Discontent regarding the institution of debtors' prisons started to grow in the 1750s, and a movement began with the circulation of a pamphlet that spoke out against the injustice of incarcerating people who could not afford to pay off their debts. There was plenty of disquiet around at this time, and the seeds of war were already planted. A profound change was imminent.

Some historians have even suggested that the rise of debt to the English crown by the colonists was a contributor to the American Revolution, seemingly as a way of debt relief for those indebted to the crown. By the 1780s, as the dust was still settling from the American War of Independence, debtors were starting to organize into societies to seek brotherhood with other debtors seeking relief. A lot of challenges remained as a result of debtors' prisons, in particular with the passage of The Pennsylvania Bankruptcy Act of 1785. The law allowed flogging and nailing of the ears of any convicted debtor. In Massachusetts during 1786 and 1787, a series of confrontations took place between desperate farmers in debt and state government authorities. The events that became known as Shays' Rebellion came to symbolize the widespread discontent manifested throughout New England during the economic depression that followed the American Revolution.[33]

Debtors' prisons in early America, though modeled after the prisons in England, typically were separate prisons or wings of a jail, so that debtors were not intermingled with the general population of criminals. Debtors' prisons of America did not discriminate based on economic class, as many affluent figures in society faced debt problems, some even jailed for not paying debts.

James Wilson, a signer of the Declaration of Independence, was incarcerated in a debtors' prison at the same time that he was an Associate Justice of the Supreme Court. The New Gaol prison was another famous debtors' prison in New York City, which once housed William Duer, a prominent attorney, member of the Continental Congress, and speculator from New York City. Duer would later die in prison after being jailed for causing the first financial scandal in America.

The fact that all classes of society were in danger of being incarcerated is where the nondiscrimination policy ended. The conditions in prison for the upper class were comparatively comfortable living with good food, while the lower classes faced overcrowding, disease, starvation, and other burdens.

The population of debtors' prisons was not diverse in early America, consisting of whites. Women were seen in debtors' prisons, but mostly as prostitutes for the upper class or wives of debtors living amongst them. While the poor of the population lived in dismal conditions, they could take a "poor man's oath," allowing them to be released from prison after thirty days upon stating under oath they had no assets or ability to pay the debt, a "privilege" not afforded the middle class and more affluent debtors. However, the upper class who owned property could escape capture if they stayed in their locked houses, where they were immune from the service of writs.

Robert Morris was a Liverpool-born American merchant who financed the American Revolution and signed the Declaration of Independence, the Articles of Confederation, and the United States Constitution. He was one of Pennsylvania's original pair of US senators and invested a considerable portion of his fortune in land shortly before the Panic of 1796–1797, which led to his bankruptcy in 1798. He evaded capture for several months on outstanding debts by staying locked in his Philadelphia home before he was arrested and incarcerated in the famous Prune Street Debtors Prison in Philadelphia. After he was released in 1801, he lived a quiet, private life in a modest home in Philadelphia until his death in 1806, never recovering his fortune.[34]

BANKRUPTCY AND DEBT

Bankruptcy played a large role in debt in early American history, as it does today. The Bankruptcy Laws in the United States are at least partially derived and influenced by the Bankruptcy and Insolvency Laws that eventually formulated in England.

Congress first exercised this power in the Bankruptcy Act of 1800. This act, which virtually copied the existing English law, provided for involuntary bankruptcies and was only available to traders (merchants). The act was repealed three years later in 1803.

The growing wave of imprisoned debtors both wealthy and poor alike only wanted relief. By the early part of the 19th century, in Philadelphia, the debtors outnumbered the violent offenders by 5 to 1, some of whom fought in the Revolutionary War, and in Boston, approximately 15 percent of the debtors in prison were women. As a result, some states began to exclude veterans and women from prison, and by 1811, Massachusetts would not imprison petty debtors.[35]

After the War of 1812, which was a costly endeavor that left a struggling economy, the amount of Americans carrying debt rose precipitously. As a result, debtors' prisons began to balloon with prisoners. To place all these debtors in prison seemed absurd, and impossible. Moreover, America was seen as a country of immigrants, and many European immigrants had come here to escape debt. Popular sentiment swelled against debtors' prisons based upon the large numbers of persons incarcerated, and the reform agenda now seemed to be on course to finally transform the debtors' prisons within the United States of America once and for all.

In 1833, Congress officially abolished imprisonment for debt in the District of Columbia and the territories, leaving the power to implement debtors' prisons in the hands of the states, many of which followed Washington's lead. Later in 1839, a Conformity Act was passed by Congress, stating federal courts would follow the law of the state where the court was seated, indirectly, banning the nationwide imprisonment for debt. However, some federal district courts interpreted the Conformity Act and exempted debts owed to the United States from the ban.

Around the same time, two short-lived federal bankruptcy laws were enacted from 1841 to 1843, and then from 1867 to 1878. A permanent federal bankruptcy law would not go into effect until 1898. Therefore, states were free to make their own bankruptcy laws without federal restriction for the vast majority of the first one hundred years after the constitution was ratified.

The Bankruptcy Act of 1898 marks the origins of bankruptcy law legislation in the United States. Unlike many prior laws in England and America, the Act provided for both voluntary and involuntary bankruptcies. Furthermore, the Act allowed debtors a discharge for most kinds of debt. Voluntary bankruptcy was allowed for everyone, not just traders.[36]

Although the Bankruptcy Act signaled the beginning of the most liberal debtor treatment in United States history, much of the law was directed not at debtor relief, but at facilitating the distribution of the debtors' property to creditors. Amendments were made to the Act after the Great Depression set in, which made the law friendlier to debtors. In 1938, the Chandler Act was passed, organizing the bankruptcy code into the various chapters that are still in existence today.

There remains today a growing concern among many American citizens that the debtors' prisons are back and functioning like never before. The colonial debtors' prisons were primarily for debt defaulters with no general prisoners mixed with them, but the ones resurfacing today are under disguised methodologies, with debt prisoners being held together with the general prisoners, hiding the ill happening behind the scenes. The emergence of these new debtors' prisons was alive and well despite concerted efforts to stop the injustice meted to several people by locking them in some debt prisons.

In the more recent American history of the 1970s and 1980s, the country started to imprison more people for lesser crimes. Experts said that this trend coincided with the rise of "mass incarceration," and that in the process, we were lowering our standards for what constituted an offense deserving of imprisonment. More broadly, these voices asserted, we were losing our sense of how serious it is to incarcerate. If we can imprison for possession of marijuana, why can't we imprison for not paying back a loan? As a result of the greater reliance on incarceration, says Karin Martin, a professor at John Jay College and an expert on criminal justice financial obligations, there was a dramatic increase in the number of statutes listing a prison term as a possible sentence for failure to repay criminal justice debt.[37]

2

OUR CONSTITUTIONAL RIGHTS AS AMERICANS

IN ADDITION TO the express US statutory provisions that speak directly to the limitations of debtors' prisons, the framers of our country enacted several constitutional provisions and amendments that can be turned to when our individual rights are infringed upon. Because of these powerful governing laws protecting our freedoms, it would seem that all Americans are duly protected from the indignities of being incarcerated merely for lack of money. There are several areas worth examining in the United States Constitution that speak directly and indirectly to the rights of debtors.

AMENDMENT 14—CITIZENSHIP RIGHTS
Section 1.
All persons born or naturalized in the United States, and subject to the jurisdiction thereof, are citizens of the United States and of the state wherein they reside. No state shall make or enforce any law which shall abridge the privileges or immunities of citizens of the United States; nor shall any state deprive any person of life, liberty, or property, without due process of law; nor deny to any person within its jurisdiction the equal protection of the laws.

Section 2.

Representatives shall be apportioned among the several states according to their respective numbers, counting the whole number of persons in each state, excluding Indians not taxed. But when the right to vote at any election for the choice of electors for President and Vice President of the United States, Representatives in Congress, the executive and judicial officers of a state, or the members of the legislature thereof, is denied to any of the male inhabitants of such state, being twenty-one years of age, and citizens of the United States, or in any way abridged, except for participation in rebellion, or other crime, the basis of representation therein shall be reduced in the proportion which the number of such male citizens shall bear to the whole number of male citizens twenty-one years of age in such state.

Section 3.

No person shall be a Senator or Representative in Congress, or elector of President and Vice President, or hold any office, civil or military, under the United States, or under any state, who, having previously taken an oath, as a member of Congress, or as an officer of the United States, or as a member of any state legislature, or as an executive or judicial officer of any state, to support the Constitution of the United States, shall have engaged in insurrection or rebellion against the same, or given aid or comfort to the enemies thereof. But Congress may by a vote of two-thirds of each House, remove such disability.

Section 4.

The validity of the public debt of the United States, authorized by law, including debts incurred for payment of pensions and bounties for services in suppressing insurrection or rebellion, shall not be questioned. But neither the United States nor any state shall assume or pay any debt or obligation incurred in aid of insurrection or rebellion against the United States, or any claim for the loss or emancipation of any slave; but all such debts, obligations and claims shall be held illegal and void.

Section 5.

The Congress shall have power to enforce, by appropriate legislation, the provisions of this article.[1]

The Fourteenth Amendment to the US Constitution, along with the Thirteenth and Fifteenth Amendments, are collectively known as the Reconstruction amendments because they were all ratified during the post-Civil War era. Of the three, the Fourteenth is the most complicated, and the one that has had the most unanticipated effects. Its broad goal was to reinforce the Civil Rights Act of 1866, which ensured that "all persons born in the United States" were citizens and were to be given "full and equal benefit of all laws." When the Civil Rights Act landed on President Andrew Johnson's desk, he vetoed it. Congress, in turn, overrode the veto, and the measure became law. Johnson, a Tennessee Democrat, repeatedly clashed with the Republican-controlled Congress. GOP leaders, fearing Johnson and Southern politicians would attempt to undo the Civil Rights Act, quickly drafted the Fourteenth Amendment, which cleared Congress in June of 1866 before going on to the states for ratification. As a condition for readmittance to the Union, the former Confederate states were required to approve the amendment, which naturally was a point of contention between Congress and Southern leaders, but within two years, the Fourteenth Amendment was formally ratified on July 28, 1868.[2]

Two sections of this Amendment stick out when considering the inequity of modern-day debtors' prisons. The first is Article one, with its mention of *due process of law* and *equal protection of the laws*. But more on that in a moment.

Section 4 of the Fourteenth Amendment essentially voided all Confederate debt accrued during the Civil War and promised that former slave owners would not be reimbursed for their freed slaves. This section was intended to protect the rights of the recently freed slaves, but 150 years later, do these sections of the Fourteenth Amendment go far enough to safeguard against people being imprisoned for debt today?

That is an important question that needs answering. In fact, it raises many more questions than it answers.

When prisoners are charged fees that they cannot afford in order to fund the very court this is subjugating them, is that a breach of our Constitutional Rights as written in the 14th Amendment?

Many people think so, including US District Judge Sarah S. Vance, who refers to this dilemma of judges imposing oppressive fines and fees on plaintiffs as an "institutional incentive."

In December 2017, this federal judge, in Orleans Parish Criminal District Court, cited in a seventy-nine-page ruling that criminal court judges do not even look into whether people facing criminal convictions can pay fees: evidence enough that there is a problem.[3]

"It is undisputed that the Judges provide no ability-to-pay inquiry, nor any further procedural safeguards, to indigent criminal defendants who are subject to imprisonment for failure to pay court debts," Justice Vance wrote. "This inquiry must involve certain procedural safeguards, especially notice to the individual of the importance of ability to pay and an opportunity to be heard on the issue. If an individual is unable to pay, then the judges must consider alternative measures before imprisoning the individual."

Under two major Supreme Court cases, Bearden v. Georgia (1983) and Turner v. Rogers (2011), criminal court judges are obligated to inquire into plaintiffs' ability to pay before their imprisonment. That being the case, you might be led to believe that in lower income communities, such fees would not be sought and collected from their residents when they find themselves before the law. In truth, that is far from the case, as exemplified in the Orleans Parish Criminal District, a district where 95 percent of arrestees cannot afford a lawyer, yet approximately $1 million collected from various fines and fees goes into its yearly budget.[4]

This paradox creates multiple problems, not the least of which is placing the judges in a very difficult position. If they do not levy fines and fees against people—most of whom are unable to pay them—there will be no money to pay staff and other necessities to run the court, and the whole system will collapse in on itself.

There's a conflict of interest when the government is collecting money that it depends on but is also supposed to enforce fair and impersonal criminal justice. So, courts should not be revenue generators, and neither should the police. This practice caught the attention of the US Department of Justice (DOJ), which in December 2016 sent out letters to state court administrators to remind them that jailing indigent people for failing to pay fines violates the US Constitution and suggested alternative practices that can address legitimate public safety needs while protecting the rights of participants in the justice system. The letter shows true leadership, challenging the phenomenon known as a modern-day debtors' prison. In one strike, the Department of Justice is telling courts across the country to guard against the illegal jailing of poor people without constitutional safeguards.[5]

The crux of the problem is clear, in that many judges simply do not adequately determine if a person can afford these additional costs to avoid being incarcerated, as is their obligation. The situation is a crisis that appears to be systemic, and not isolated to specific jurisdictions or certain geographic regions of the country.

Around the same time of Justice Vance's proclamation in New Orleans, a federal court issued a preliminary injunction halting Michigan's system for suspending driver's licenses upon nonpayment of traffic tickets due to constitutional concerns. And days later, the Mississippi Department of Public Safety agreed to reinstate the driver's licenses of all those suspended for non-payment of court fines and fees.[6]

These examples of infringement of the rights of individuals who cannot pay fines and court costs have been going on for a long time, and they continue to be a concern for many people even today. It is obvious that the rights of all Americans are spelled out clearly in the Articles and Amendments of the Constitution, but the responsibility of interpreting these laws falls into the hands of a relatively few men and women who must render court decisions that are fair and just.

Ultimately, debtors' prisons are not only unfair and senseless, but they are also illegal. Imprisoning someone because he or she cannot afford to pay court-imposed fines or fees violates the Fourteenth Amendment promises of due process and equal protection under the law.

Bearden v. Georgia

Ironically, colonial Georgia was originally created as a place for debtors to escape the cycle of incarceration and debt.[7] Then along came Danny Bearden, a young man from Tunnel Hill, a small town in northern Georgia that had a population of under a thousand people in 1980 when Bearden was indicted for the felonies of burglary and theft by receiving stolen property. He did not enter a judgement of guilt, having further proceedings deferred, and the first-time offender was sentenced to three years probation with the stipulation that he pay a fine of $500, plus an additional $250 in restitution. While Bearden managed to pay some of his fine initially, having to borrow some money to do so, he subsequently lost his job, and with no income, he could not pay the remainder. When Bearden informed the probation department that he would not have the funds to pay the remaining balance, the State of Georgia revoked his probation for failure to pay and sentenced Danny to the remaining term of probation in jail. Unable to afford an attorney, he was appointed one by the state. Jim Lohr was young and fresh out of law school, but he had done his homework on the case and took it all the way to the highest court in the land. On appeal to the State Courts of Georgia, Danny argued that to imprison him to jail for failure to pay the fines violated the Fourteenth Amendment's Equal Protection Clause. The Supreme Court granted Danny certiorari, which is an order by which a higher court reviews a decision of a lower court.

In summary, the Supreme Court unanimously held that Bearden's imprisonment violated his Fourteenth Amendment rights to "fundamental fairness." In other words, someone could not be imprisoned simply for failure to pay through no fault of his or her own. As our Supreme Court put it, revoking the probation of a person who, "through no fault of his own, is unable to make restitution will not make restitution suddenly forthcoming."[8] The Court outlined guidelines for States to consider when conducting probation revocation, proceedings. If a person "willfully" refuses to pay or fails to make bona fide efforts to acquire the resources to pay, a court may revoke probation and imprison the person within the range of its sentencing authority.[9] If the defendant makes bona fide efforts to pay the debt and still could not pay, a Court must consider "alternative measures of punishment other than imprisonment," and only if those alternative measures are "not adequate to meet the state's interest in punishment and deterrence may the court imprison" a person who has made bona fide efforts to attempt to pay.[10]

By now, debtors' prisons should well be a thing of the past. *Bearden* should have seen to that. But has it?

Not necessarily.

The decision from the 1983 landmark Supreme Court case, *Bearden v. Georgia*, affirmed that incarcerating indigent debtors was unconstitutional under the Fourteenth Amendment's Equal Protection clause, and it held that a judge must first consider whether the defendant has the ability to pay but "willfully" refuses. However, the Supreme Court didn't tell courts how to determine what it means to "willfully" not pay. So it was left to judges to make sometimes difficult calculations. Despite this high court ruling more than three decades ago, an NPR News recent investigation found there continue to be wide discrepancies in how judges make those decisions. And every day, people go to jail because they failed to pay their court debts.[11]

Notable Cases

In 1970, the United States Supreme Court took the case of Willie Williams from the State of Illinois. On August 16, 1967, Willie was convicted of petty theft and received the maximum sentence allowed by state law: one year in jail, a $500 fine, and $5.00 in court costs. Part of the judgment stated that if Willie was in default of the fine and costs after he served the one year in jail, he was to remain incarcerated and "work off" the fine and costs at the rate of $5.00 per day. *Williams v. Illinois.* The effect of Willie's sentence would be to keep a person who could not afford to pay financial obligations jail an additional 101 days to pay $505.00 above and beyond the original one-year sentence.

While still in jail, Willie petitioned the sentencing court to vacate the requirement to extend jail time due to his inability to pay fines and costs. He asked to be released to obtain a job to pay the financial obligations. The Illinois Court denied Willie's petition. The basis for the denial was that his argument was not ripe because he was still serving his jail sentence and his financial ability could change. Mr. Williams didn't give up and took his appeal to the Illinois Supreme Court.

The higher state court denied his appeal once again. Notable in the higher court's decision was that they found no violation of equal protection when an indigent person is jailed to satisfy payment of a fine. Williams then took his appeal to United States Supreme Court. The Court agreed to hear his appeal. Chief Justice Burger wrote the decision for the Court. The Court vacated the State Court judgment and in doing so found that the Equal Protection Clause of the Fourteenth Amendment requires that the statutory ceiling placed on imprisonment for an offense be the same for all defendants regardless of their economic status. In coming to their decision, the Court relied on their previous decision in *Griffin v. Illinois*. States have a public interest in protecting their citizens and punishing people who commit crimes. However, once they have satisfied that interest in penalizing, the States may not then discriminate against a certain class of defendants and imprison them beyond the statutory maximum solely because they can't pay. The Court makes note that the "constitutional imperatives of the Equal Protection Clause must have priority over the comfortable convenience of the *status quo*."

A year later, the Supreme Court granted certiorari in the case of *Tate v. Short*. Tate had nine convictions for traffic offenses in Houston, Texas, which totaled $425.00. The petitioner could not afford to pay the fines and was sent to a prison farm to work off the fines at a rate of $5.00 per day. It would take Tate eighty-five days of jail time to pay the fines in full. After twenty-one days at the farm, Tate filed a habeas corpus petition based on the fact that he was unable to pay the fines. The State Court in Texas denied his petition.

The Supreme Court agreed to take the case and reversed the State Court, relying on the case of Willie Williams. The Court realized that Tate is different in the respect that it involves offenses punishable by fine only. The petitioner's imprisonment is equally discriminatory as it is in the *Williams* case, because it was solely due to the offender's inability to pay. The Court notes that the like *Williams*, the State has a valid interest in the collection and enforcing of the payment of fines. In this case, there is no penal objective of the State, and the jail sentence is imposed solely to increase the State's revenues. The Court states that Tate's imprisonment does not aid the collection of revenue, but it actually does the reverse. It "saddles the State with the cost of feeding and housing him for the period of his imprisonment."

AMENDMENT 5—TRIAL AND PUNISHMENT, COMPENSATION FOR TAKINGS

No person shall be held to answer for a capital, or otherwise infamous crime, unless on a presentment or indictment of a Grand Jury, except in cases arising in the land or naval forces, or in the Militia, when in actual service in time of War or public danger; nor shall any person be subject for the same offense to be twice put in jeopardy of life or limb; nor shall be compelled in any criminal case to be a witness against himself, nor be deprived of life, liberty, or property, without due process of law; nor shall private property be taken for public use, without just compensation.[12]

While the Fourteenth Amendment of the United States Constitution reads similarly—". . . nor shall any State deprive any person of life, liberty, or property, without due process of law . . ."—the Fifth Amendment reads in pertinent part that "No person shall be . . . deprived of life, liberty, or property, without due process of law." Both are known as the Due Process clause and interpreted similarly by the United States Supreme Court, even though the Fourteenth Amendment applies to the States and the Fifth Amendment applies to the federal government.

The Fifth Amendment contains the Due Process guarantee, which means that government action must never be improper or unfair. The government must follow the rules when seeking to deprive the "life, liberty or property" of a person. However, strictly following the law does not always ensure people are treated fairly or with justice. Therefore, the Fifth Amendment also requires that substantive due process be followed. Meaning the government cannot just act fairly, it must apply the law fairly to all people. Government shall not single out one particular person or group for better or worse treatment.

The Fifth Amendment to the United States Constitution, as a provision of the Bill of Rights, enumerates several of the most important protections of persons accused of crimes under the American criminal justice system. These protections include: protection from being prosecuted for crimes unless first legally indicted by a Grand Jury; protection from "double jeopardy"—being prosecuted more than once for the same criminal act; protection from "self-incrimination"—being forced to testify or provide evidence against one's self; and protection against being deprived of life, liberty, or property without "due process of law" or just compensation.

The Fifth Amendment, as part of the original twelve provisions of the Bill of Rights, was submitted to the states by Congress on September 25, 1789, and was ratified on December 15, 1791.[13]

In the context of debtors' rights, the Fifth Amendment is used quite regularly. Many people believe the right to self-incrimination is reserved for criminal proceedings. However, debtors are using its protections in civil and bankruptcy proceedings, as well. In fact, the Fifth Amendment self-incrimination privilege may be asserted in any proceeding where questions are asked of a witness that may be incriminatory in nature. The Court, in *In re Connelly*, suggested the Fifth Amendment privilege may be invoked when a witness is compelled to give testimony in court that is incriminatory in nature.[14] Individuals exercising the Fifth Amendment right in civil proceedings are not required to make a knowing and intelligent waiver, as is done in criminal proceedings. In civil proceedings, witnesses may assert the privilege as long as it is done in a timely manner. Therefore, an individual invoking the privilege must do so directly after the question is asked.[15] Additionally, the witness must assert the privilege after each question is asked; blanket assertions are not permissible.[16] The Sixth Circuit Court has held that a debtor has the burden of proving that there is a real danger of incrimination when invoking the privilege.[17] At least one bankruptcy court was a little more lenient than requiring the threat of incrimination be shown and instead ruled a debtor must only show that the information requested will provide the evidence needed for prosecution.[18] In bankruptcy proceedings, debtors waive the privilege when they fail to assert it, and the answers given to incriminating questions can be used against them, both criminally and civilly. As a consequence, jail time is a possibility for providing incriminating responses to questions where debtors could have invoked the fifth amendment.[19]

AMENDMENT 8

Excessive bail shall not be required, nor excessive fines imposed, nor cruel and unusual punishments inflicted.

The Eighth Amendment's states that "excessive fines" not be "imposed," but what exactly does that mean? "Excessive fines" is certainly a very subjective term and is open to interpretation. Historically, the Excessive Fines Clause of the Eighth Amendment can appropriately be understood as encoding two complementary, but distinct, constitutional principles: "(1) a proportionality principle, linking the penalty to the offense, and (2) an additional limiting principle linking the penalty imposed to the offender's economic status and circumstances."[20]

Interestingly, the Eighth Amendment was inspired by the case in England of Titus Oates, who was tried by the court system for multiple acts of perjury, which led to the executions of many people whom Oates had wrongly accused of grave crimes. The subsequent punishment of Oates involved ordinary penalties that were imposed in a brutal and excessive manner. In England, the outlawing of cruel and unusual punishments effectively limited the discretion of judges and required the authoritative body to adhere to precedents. The state of Virginia was the first to adopt the provision of the English Bill of Rights, for it was included in the Virginia Declaration of Rights of 1776. The Eighth Amendment is a part of the Bill of Rights, which are the first ten Amendments to the United States Constitution and the framework to elucidate upon the freedoms of the individual.[21]

Simple and to the point. For the purpose of our discussion, the Eighth Amendment was enacted to ensure that people did not languish in jail.

The Eighth Amendment is perhaps most often mentioned in the context of the death penalty. It forbids forms of punishments entirely while outlawing other forms of punishments that are excessive when related to the crime in question or compared to the competence of the aggressor. The Supreme Court outlawed public dissecting, burning a perpetrator alive, drawing and quartering, or disemboweling, regardless of the crime. The Supreme Court also outlawed the execution of any individuals under the age of eighteen, or any individual who is mentally handicapped. The Supreme Court ruled that it was unconstitutional to fine individual excessively based on their economic or financial standing. Additionally, the Supreme Court, through previous provisions instituted by the English Bill of Rights, stated that excessive bail is not required; however, the Eighth Amendment also states that bail may be denied if the charges are grave and serious enough to terminate the option.[22]

In 1998, the Supreme Court took up the case of *United States v. Bajakajian* and held that forfeiture was an "excessive" fine in violation of the Eighth Amendment.[23] Since *Bajakajian*, the lower courts, for the most part, have disregarded a defendant's inability to pay a fine as a "relevant consideration in the context of the Eighth Amendment."[24] One lower court that has tackled the emergence of the Excessive Fines Clause is the First Circuit. The Court has gone some way toward resurrecting a foundational, but today the "largely forgotten principle of English law known as *salvo contenemento suo* (translated as "saving his contentment," or livelihood)."[25] This principle, derived from the Magna Carta, had become firmly established as a fundamental principle in common law by the 17th and 18th centuries: "The principle required, among other things, that a defendant not be fined an amount that exceeded his ability to pay."[26] The history suggests that the English Bill of Rights' forbidding of "excessive fines" was "intended—at least in part—to reaffirm this principle."[27]

Today, people accused of a crime in this country need to appear for a trial. Applied effectively, the Eighth Amendment should balance the interests of the government to ensure that a person appear in court and that the person have the right to remain free while awaiting trial. The system of bail is the compromise between the two interests. Ordinarily, bail is an amount of money deposited with that the court to assure a person appearance. If accused persons meet all their obligations, the money is returned to them at the end of the trial. There is also a prohibition against excessive fines imposed, for example, fines imposed to punish a person for not appearing in court. Much later, the United State Supreme Court in 2001 ruled that the excessive fines provision applied to the states in *Cooper Industries vs. Letherman Tool Group, Inc.* You will see in later chapters how the current state of the bail system has contributed to the overcrowding of prisons nationwide.

Article I, Section 8, Clause 4—The Bankruptcy Clause

The Congress shall have Power To ... establish ... uniform Laws on the subject of Bankruptcies throughout the United States.

Taking the historical context into perspective, there is no wonder the framers of the Constitution were compelled to include the Bankruptcy Clause in Article I. Section 8, Clause 4 states, "Congress shall have power . . . to establish . . . uniform Laws on the subject of Bankruptcies throughout the United States."

The Bankruptcy Clause of the Constitution was one of Congress's several delegated powers in Article I, Section 8, which were designed to encourage the development of a commercial republic and to temper the excesses of pro-debtor state legislation that proliferated under the Articles of Confederation. Both state legislation and state courts tended to use debtor-creditor laws to redistribute money from out-of-state and urban creditors to rural agricul-tural interests. Under the Articles of Confederation, the states alone gov-erned debtor-creditor relations, and that led to diverse and contradictory state laws. It was unclear, for instance, whether a state law that purported to discharge a debtor of a debt prohibited the creditor from trying to collect the debt in another state. Prodebtor state laws also interfered with the reliability of contracts, and creditors confronted still further obstructions in trying to use state courts to collect their judgments, especially when debtors absconded to other states to avoid collection.[28]

In a free, democratic society, bankruptcy is a topic that is important to the individual as well as to society as a whole. Regulations need to be concise and comprehensive to protect everyone. The ways in which bankruptcy can jeop-ardize individuals freedoms will be addressed in a later chapter, but it is worth noting how the Constitution was framed regarding this issue.

A coherent and consistent bankruptcy regime for merchants was also required for the United States to flourish as a commercial republic. The framers were so convinced of the need for a national power over bankruptcy that there was hardly any debate over the issue at the Constitutional Con-vention. The Bankruptcy Clause helped to further the goals of uniformity and predictability within the federalist system. As James Madison observed in *The Federalist* No. 42, "The power of establishing uniform laws of bank-ruptcy is so intimately connected with the regulation of commerce, and will prevent so many frauds where the parties or their property may lie or be removed into different States, that the expediency of it seems not likely to be drawn into question." As Madison suggests, there was little debate over and little opposition to the Bankruptcy Clause at the Constitutional Conven-tion. Although state law continued to govern most routine debtor-creditor relations, Congress had the authority to override state laws dealing with insolvency. Following ratification of the Constitution, the mercantile north-eastern states spearheaded the movement for a national bankruptcy law. The first bankruptcy law was passed under the Federalists in 1800, but it lasted only until 1803. Other bankruptcy laws existed from 1841 to 1843 and from 1867 to 1878. The first permanent bankruptcy law was enacted in 1898 and remained in effect, with amendments, until being replaced with a comprehensive new law in 1978, the essential structure of which continues today.[29]

After the ratification of the Constitution, it remained unclear where the line between the state and federal power should be drawn. English law relied upon a traditional distinction between "bankruptcies" on the one hand and "insolvency" on the other. Under English law, only merchants and traders could be declared "bankrupt," which enabled them to have their debts discharged upon the satisfaction of certain requirements. By contrast, nonmerchants had to seek refuge under "insolvency" laws, which did little more than release a debtor from debtors' prison but did not discharge the debtor from his indebtedness. Thus, many understood the Constitution's grant of power to Congress to regulate "bankruptcies" as creating federal power to regulate only with respect to merchants and traders and not with respect to those individuals traditionally subject to "insolvency" laws, which remained under state control. Others argued that this traditional distinction had disappeared by the mid-18th century and that by the time of the Constitution, the terms became interchangeable, so as to give Congress the power to regulate all insolvent debtors.[30]

In 1819, the Supreme Court held in *Sturges v. Crowninshield* that the use of the term *bankruptcy* in the Constitution did not limit Congress's jurisdiction, thereby permitting Congress to regulate both of these realms. In *Ogden v. Saunders* (1827), the Court further restricted the states' concurrent power, prohibiting the discharge of debts owed to citizens of another state, but permitting discharge of debts owed to a citizen of the same state so long as the law operated prospectively so as not to impair contract obligations. Still, the original understanding of the Bankruptcy Clause placed several clear constraints on Congress's authority to regulate on the subject of debtor-creditor relations. First, Congress's power under the Bankruptcy Clause is limited to the adjustment of the debts of *insolvent* debtors and their creditors and does not extend to the general regulation of debtor-creditor law. Previous bankruptcy laws required that the debtor be insolvent as a condition for bankruptcy, but the current Bankruptcy Code contains no such limitation. Second, Congress's bankruptcy power was limited to the adjustment of relations between a debtor and his creditors and does not extend to the protection or benefit of third parties, except to the extent that such protection is ancillary to the adjustment of the debts of an insolvent debtor. This original limitation is also ineffective today.[31]

The Bankruptcy Code thus represents a tenuous accommodation between federal and state law. Most of the nonbankruptcy law that governs debtor-creditor relations remains state law, and federal bankruptcy law honors these state-law substantive entitlements unless federal law and policy expressly preempt them. Moreover, the Bankruptcy Code expressly incorporates some elements of state law into the Code itself, such as in the treatment of a debtor's property exemptions. This interaction between state and federal law guarantees that creditors and debtors will be treated differently depending on the state that determines their rights. At the same time, any bankruptcy legislation enacted by Congress must also be "uniform . . . throughout the United States." In *Hanover National Bank v. Moyses* (1902), the Supreme Court held that this "personal" nonuniformity in treatment among individuals was permissible, so long as "geographical" uniformity was preserved. Thus, debtors and creditors in *different states* may receive different treatment, as long as the debtors and creditors within the *same state* are treated the same. The "uniformity" requirement does, however, forbid "private" bankruptcy laws that affect only particular debtors.[32]

Regardless of all these protections, today many thousands of people are currently in jail or prison for failure to pay some form of monetary obligation. While the debtors' prisons of the past mainly involved the jailing of a person for failing to pay a commercial debt, the new debtors' prisons involve both criminal and civil law. Incarceration may stem from crime, taxes, child support, civil collection matters, licensing fees, alimony, and tort. Additionally, taxes, fines, penalties, and student loans are part of the list of potential reasons why a person could go to jail.

It cannot be overlooked that in some parts of the country today, defendants are not given a judicial hearing until their debts are paid, an unconstitutional practice that is frequently framed as a routine administrative matter. And to make matters worse, an increasing number of states and localities look to close budget gaps through fees and fines accessed through the criminal justice system. The scenario has created a cottage industry of for-profit probation companies, which is a topic we will talk more about later in the book.[33]

Throughout this chapter, we touched on the Constitutional protections afforded to all Americans through the all-important document known as the United States Constitution, as well as some important landmark cases of the United States Supreme Court that have helped interpret the Constitution and its amendments. We have heard terms such as Equal Protection, Excessive Bail, and Due Process. One topic we fail to see is how the Constitution protects American citizens from the power of the government itself. The majority of Americans do not have the resources, monetary and otherwise, to fight for their rights and prove their innocence in the criminal justice system. When faced with allegations of a criminal offense, the government is coming down on you with all their resources to prove a crime was committed. They have unlimited resources. Most Americans don't; they are working paycheck to paycheck, many without the resources to obtain a lawyer and do an investigation to prove their innocence. The government has law enforcement and the all the assets of the government to bring a world of hurt upon an individual.

One of the authors of this book found himself in that exact position. A father of two young children, working as a lawyer who had thousands to pay off from student loan debt, trying to live the American Dream. In 2008–09, he came face-to-face with the strong arm of the federal government and an uphill climb. While he woke up to take his kids to school each day and go to work to pay bills, the Federal Government woke up each day to try to prove he committed financial crimes.

3
THE MIDDLE-CLASS DEBT CRISIS

WHILE FEDERAL LAW passed in 1833 stipulated that a person could not be jailed for having outstanding debt, and *Bearden v. Georgia* held that a local government can only imprison or jail someone for not paying a fine if it can be shown by means of a hearing that the person in question could have paid it but "willfully" chose not to do so, debtors' prisons have not disappeared in this country. The fact is that today every state has its own set of rules when it comes to debt. For example, in some states, you could be jailed for contempt of court for failing to appear in court over a debt dispute. A few states will imprison a parent who has fallen behind on child support. In modern society, debt is inescapable, and having credit is, in fact, acceptable and necessary for personal economic sustainability. Having good credit is much sought after and is just a means of accumulating debt.

How much debt is too much?

The answer might not be the same for every individual; many Americans owe more now than they ever have before, with overall US household debt increasing by 11 percent in the past decade.[1]

This increasing debt load isn't simply a case of overindulging on luxuries and living beyond one's means. The truth is, many people use credit cards to cover necessities when their income no longer goes as far as it used to, and they do not overspend on frivolities, such as smartphone apps, treating them-selves to specialty coffee, or even unaffordable vacations. Rather, income growth is being dwarfed by a rapid increase in food, housing, and medical costs, the largest expenses for consumers. Household income has grown by 28 percent in the past thirteen years, but the cost of living has gone up 30 percent in that period. Medical costs increased by 57 percent and food and beverage prices by 36 percent in that same span.[2] These increases have made it exceptionally challenging for many families to make ends meet without relying on credit cards and loans.

A basic principle is that when the cost of living outpaces income growth, debt increases.[3]

Taking on debt to cover the gap between income and expenses is a short-term fix with costly long-term results, according to Sean McQuay, a credit and banking expert.

To see how you compare to the average household in America, take a look at these 2017 numbers:

	Total owed by average US household carrying this debt	Total debt owed by US consumers
Credit cards	$16,748	$779 billion
Mortgages	$176,222	$8.48 trillion
Auto Loans	$28,948	$1.16 trillion
Student Loans	$49,905	$1.31 trillion[4]

These are just statistics, however, and do not tell the whole story. What is most significant is that the numbers represent real people, and one face might be easily recognizable by just looking in the mirror.

Arguably, the biggest burdens weighing on the American middle class is debt, and as it continues to grow, it threatens the prosperity of more and more families. Most do not know the peril they are in until it is too late. Any unexpected expense—a tax, fine, or medical bill—could put you and your family at risk of losing everything: credit rating, car, home, ability to make a living, even your freedom.

It's something that is hard to believe because you don't think it is going to happen to you if you are among the 88 percent of Americans who consider themselves among the middle class. According to Credit Suisse, 25 percent of Americans have a negative net worth.[5] What that means is that if you have no debt and ten dollars in your pocket, then you have a greater net worth than a quarter of all Americans. Credit Suisse also estimates that half of the world has a net worth less than $3,210, and a large chunk of Americans can't make that cut because their net worth is negative.[6]

How could something like that happen?

Debt has become the American Way, with people going deeply into debt for buying things that they can't afford simply to keep up with the Joneses. And it's too easy. The US financial system encourages debt by keeping interest rates at effectively zero. You can borrow money in many cases for less interest than you can save, which is especially the situation in Europe, where some banks are actually paying people to borrow money.[7]

It could further be considered that for much of the past century, easier access to credit has benefited most Americans. It helped them buy what many see as the necessities of middle-class life, such as a home, a car, an education. Those assets, in turn, gave them the stability and earning power they needed to build wealth. Regular mortgage payments acted as a form of saving, making home ownership almost synonymous with financial security.[8]

US economic growth continued for a long while due to consumption increases. For a long time, America's economic growth was sustained by the powerful force of increased consumption paid for by earning increases for middle and working classes. This growth could not be sustained forever, and at the time Ronald Reagan was elected president of the United States, the consumption continued even though wages began to stagnate. Homeownership still defines the American dream, so mortgage debt easily becomes the biggest liability for most American families. It stand to reason that with increased debt, there is decreased personal savings, leaving little or no liquid capital to pay for unexpected expenses of any kind.

After thirty years, as this elastic band of credit reached its limit and could not be stretched any further, it finally snapped in 2007. Consumption dropped, and as the bottom fell out of housing market, while mortgage-backed securities and derivatives lost significant value, many homes and jobs were lost. America was in the midst of what has become known as the Great Recession, a term that represents the sharp decline in economic activity during the late 2000s, which is considered the largest downturn since the Great Depression. The term "Great Recession" applies to both the US recession, officially lasting from December 2007 to June 2009, and the ensuing global recession in 2009. The economic slump began when the US housing market went from boom to bust and large amounts of mortgage-backed securities and derivatives lost significant value.[9]

HOME IS WHERE THE DEBT IS

With today's economy seemingly on the mend, it appears that we may be going back to our lend-and-spend ways that started us down this destructive economic path in the first place. Cutting interest rates and generous banks loans have gotten the credit merry-go-round going again, and if we don't learn from our past mistakes, we are surely bound to repeat them. It's a surreal economic strategy, because, while the proximate cause of the Great Recession was the collapse of borrowing in 2007 and 2008, the ultimate cause was the growth of unsustainable debt over many years, culminating in a doubling of debt between 2000 and 2007. Leverage can get you out of a ditch, but it was leverage that got us into that ditch in the first place. Debt is no sin, and borrowing to finance investments that will pay off in the future is a smart thing to do. Stretching out the payments for things that last a long time, such as homes, cars, or appliances, can also make a lot of sense.

However, borrowing to pay for immediate consumption can spell financial ruin.[10]

Some economists have noted that in recent years, our political leaders and the public have been worried about the wrong debt. They've been intently focused on reducing the federal government's debt, not on household debt. It's become a big debate about whether the nation can survive with a government debt-to-GDP ratio above 90 percent, but there has been almost no discussion about what it means for private-sector debt to total 240 percent of GDP.[11]

While the broad outline of how private debt destroyed the economy has been known for years, economists like Thomas Palley and Dean Baker predicted that the growth in private debt was unsustainable. Since the Great Recession, there's been a flurry of research digging deeper into the details, giving us a better idea of just how it played out. The Great Recession resulted in the loss of eight million jobs between 2007 and 2009. More than four million homes were lost to foreclosures. Is it a coincidence that the United States witnessed a dramatic rise in household debt in the years before the recession, and that the total amount of debt for American households doubled between 2000 and 2007 to $14 trillion?[12]

Atif Mian and Amir Sufi's epic *House of Debt* shows that the recession wasn't a banking crisis that could be easily fixed by bailing out banks so they could lend again. Instead, the crisis was caused by the protracted accumulation of debt by households until it reached a breaking point. And when households could no longer service their debts, it turned into a banking crisis.[13]

Research by economists Barry Z. Cynamon and Steven M. Fazzar links stagnant income growth for middle-class families from the mid-1980s to 2007 and the explosive growth in their debts. They show that middle-class families were able to maintain their consumption growth only by taking on more debt, which they mostly used to buy homes. As long as house prices were rising, their net worth was increasing, and it seemed sensible to spend some of those riches. Once the credit spigot was turned off and their wealth was destroyed, consumption by middle-class families plummeted. The anemic recovery can be largely explained by the retrenchment of the middle class. However, richer families—those in the top 5 percent—cut back their spending only temporarily, because their consumption was based on steadily growing incomes, not on debt.[14]

This matters because we're treating symptoms, not the disease. We still have an economy that relies too much on leverage by middle-class families, who have made some progress in reducing their debt burden since the recession, but not nearly enough. Recent data show that the middle class is once again borrowing, chiefly for education and cars. While the cost of servicing these debts has fallen to a record low thanks to low interest rates, middle-class families remain vulnerable if interest rates rise significantly.[15] This also leaves the economy susceptible, because the correlation between the middle-class spending and the economy is critical. The rich, incongruously, do not spend enough to keep the economy moving forward. Of course, rich people are comparatively few in number, while at the same time analysis shows that the top 1 percent of people now own half of the world's wealth.[16]

The reality is that our economy can only grow if the middle class is working and spending money, but the middle class cannot spend if there are no jobs, or incomes are flat and if they are burdened with debt. Incomes of the middle class need to rise in order to stave off a long period of stagnation in the US economy. The fear that the situation is even more perilous than that is not without the presence of some very disheartening signs forecasting the death of the middle class.[17]

Numbers for 2015 released by the Social Security Administration reveal that 51 percent of all workers in the United States make less than $30,000 a year. It does not seem feasible that a family could support itself on $2,500 a month, yet more than half of all workers in this country have to get by on just that. Some of the other eye-opening statistics include these:

- 38 percent of all American workers made less than $20,000 last year
- 62 percent of all American workers made less than $40,000 last year
- 71 percent of all American workers made less than $50,000 last year[18]

It has been estimated that it takes approximately $50,000 a year to support a middle-class lifestyle for a family of four in the US today, so the fact that 71 percent of all workers make less than that amount shows how difficult it is for families that try to get by with just a single breadwinner. Working a full-time job that pays $10 an hour would earn a worker approximately $20,000, which says a lot about our economy and the quality of jobs available to the working class.[19] In many families, both the husband and the wife are working as hard as they can, but it is still not enough. Needless to say, a tremendous squeeze has been put on the middle class who are living paycheck to paycheck. With nearly eight million working-age Americans unemployed, and another 95 million working-age Americans who are considered "not in the labor force," the crisis is even greater.[20] With each passing day, more Americans are losing their spots in the middle class, and this has pushed government dependence to an all-time high. According to the US Census Bureau, 49 percent of all Americans now live in a home that receives money from the government each month. So many middle-class families are barely scraping by and only sinking deeper into debt.[21] Any unforeseen expenditure or cost-of-living increase can have a profound effect on their lives and welfare. Even a small fine or court fee can prove too much, given how such charges can rapidly increase if they are not paid on time, and it is these very working-class people who are in danger becoming a statistic of a different kind by finding themselves locked up in America's new debtors' prisons.

DEBT COLLECTION WOES

According to figures by the Urban Institute, a Washington, DC-based think tank, more than one-third of Americans, roughly 35 percent, have debts and unpaid bills that have been turned over to collection agencies. These consumers had fallen behind on payments owed to various creditors, including the banks for their mortgages and car loans.[22] Five percent of people with a credit file have a report of past due debt, indicating they are between thirty and 180 days late on a nonmortgage payment.[23] A medical or utility bill that is more than 180 days past-due can be placed in collections. Student debt was also among the financial shortfalls of these individuals.[24] Even smaller delinquent accounts, like past-due gym memberships and cell phone contracts can wind up at a collection agency, an action that can hinder more than a person's credit scores.

Caroline Ratcliffe, a senior fellow at the Urban Institute, stated, "Roughly, every third person you pass on the street is going to have debt in collections. It can tip employers' hiring decisions, or whether or not you get that apartment."[25]

Collection agencies are a relatively new enterprise, and before they came about, it was entirely the creditor's responsibility to recover the money owed to them. The necessity to collect debt existed long before currency, even before the invention of money, when the bartering of goods or services in return for other goods or services often led to the creation of debt as one of the parties failed to deliver on their end of the exchange.

The earliest recording of how debt was dealt with goes back to 3,000 BC and the ancient civilization of Sumer, a region of ancient Mesopotamia, now modern-day Iraq. Chronicles explain how a debtor was forced to work for the creditor until such time that his physical labor had repaid the debt. In some cases, it could take years to repay the debt, which could even be passed on to the following generation of the debtor's family. Debt slaves became common throughout many ancient civilizations, though some of the more liberal early societies introduced forms of debt forgiveness or allowed debts to be discharged after a specific period. Among Abrahamic religions, lending was discouraged, and creditors were prohibited from seeking to collect debts. Debt slavery continued for many hundreds of years and was known as debt bondage by the Greek and Roman Empires. The practice was widespread and considered quite normal by the great classical empires. The poor and those who suffered financial burdens could even voluntarily choose to enter bondage as a debtor to avoid some of the more violent alternatives that could be imposed on them. Many, however, considered indentured labor to be the most severe form of debt bondage, and it involved a legally signed contract that often contained many clauses that favored the creditor over the debtor and forced the debtor to repay the debt many times over or leave him in continual poverty.[26]

During the Middle Ages, when laws were introduced by many countries to deal with debt collection, a creditor could summon the debtor to Court and seek a Judgment against him. A bailiff would then be instructed by the Court to enter the debtor's premises and remove goods of value before delivering them to the creditor. The bailiff would also remove, or more appropriately pillage, far more than necessary to repay the debt, sometimes even forcing the debtor to hand over the deed to his property, while little if any of the bounty seized was ever delivered to the creditor.

In more modern times, debt recovery resulted in debtors being imprisoned, as detailed in Chapter 1 of this book. Once debtors' prisons were done away with, creditors had no solid recourse against delinquent debtors. If there was collateral involved in the debt, such as a mortgage, the creditor could take the property in order to indemnify themselves. Seizing property was often the case during the Great Depression, when banks foreclosed on homes at an astounding rate, only to leave them empty and rotting, as no one could afford to buy them up. This practice gave the banks a bad reputation and didn't help anyone gain any financial footing along the way.

Today, if a debt is unsecured, such as medical bills or education expenses, there is no way for the creditor to collect on his investment if the debtor has no money. Even if he receives a judgment against the debtor in court, everything hinges on the debtor being able to pay the judgment. The only thing a lender can do is try to extend credit only to those who stand a good chance of paying it back. With the advent of collection agencies, the creditor has the upper hand once again. There are several types of collection agencies. Among the more common include first-party agencies, which are often subsidiaries of the company to which the debt is owed, and third-party agencies, which are separate companies contracted by a company to collect debts on their behalf for a fee. There are also debt buyers, independent companies that purchase the debt at a percentage of its value, then attempt to collect it themselves.

According to the Urban Institute, the average debt owed by an individual reported to a collection agency is $5,178, and the share of Americans in collections remains relatively constant, even as the country as a whole has whittled down the size of its credit card debt since the official end of the Great Recession in the middle of 2009. In fact, credit card debt has reached its lowest level in more than a decade, according to the American Bankers Association. People increasingly pay off balances each month. Just 2.44 percent of card accounts are overdue by thirty days or more, versus the fifteen-year average of 3.82 percent. Yet roughly the same percentage of people are still getting reported for unpaid bills, according to the Urban Institute study performed in conjunction with researchers from the Consumer Credit Research Institute. Their figures nearly match the 36.5 percent of people in collections reported by a 2004 Federal Reserve analysis. The collections industry has become a boon to the American economy, employing 140,000 workers who recover $50 billion each year, according to a separate study published by the Federal Reserve's Philadelphia bank branch.[27]

Here is a partial breakdown of figures identified in the study: Healthcare-related bills account for 37.9 percent of all debts collected, as per a new report that was commissioned by the Association of Credit Collection Professionals; student loan debt accounts for another 25.2 percent; credit card debt amounts to 10.1 percent of collections; and the remainder of collections go to local governments, telecoms, retailers, and public utility companies.

The delinquent debt is overwhelmingly concentrated in Southern and Western states, with Texas cities have a largest share of their populations being reported to collection agencies, such as Dallas (44.3 percent), El Paso (44.4 percent), Houston (43.7 percent), San Antonio (44.5 percent), and McAllen (51.7 percent).[28]

Other cities have populations that have largely managed to repay their bills on time. Just 20.1 percent of Minneapolis residents have debts in collection. Boston, Honolulu, and San Jose, CA, are similarly low. Only about 20 percent of Americans with credit records have any debt at all. Yet high debt levels don't always lead to more delinquencies, since the debt largely comes from mortgages. An average San Jose resident has $97,150 in total debt, with 84 percent of it tied to a mortgage. But because incomes and real estate values are higher in the technology hub, those residents are less likely to be delinquent. By contrast, the average person in the Texas city of McAllen has only $23,546 in debt, yet more than half of the population has debt in collections, more than anywhere else in the United States.[29]

MIDDLE CLASS UNDER ASSAULT

Eric Salazar, the Texas and Florida manager for GreenPath, a credit counseling agency, pointed to several major factors that were driving delinquencies. For one, many of the workers in collections have low-paying jobs, including construction and service industry jobs. They have minimal education regarding their finances, according to GreenPath. "There is not the income growth to save and they have to make survival decisions," Salazar told AP. "You make the decision to pay for the roof over your head and to feed your family and that's all you can afford to do." He also said the states most affected are homes to retirees who live on fixed incomes and may often struggle to pay some bills, especially medical bills.[30]

Their website indicated that 24,750,000 American households have relied on payday loans or other fringe services and that 53,831,250 families do not have three months, savings. Organizations like GreenPath devise action plans for individual and families to improve the financial stability of the household, customizing budgets and offering advice on credit and debt issues. Such organizations can be beneficial to middle-class people struggling to keep their heads above water. They are not for rich people, assisting them to get richer. They are for average Americans to keep as much of their hard-earned money as possible and to be sure they have enough savings to meet their future needs.[31]

A study by the Hamilton Project, a think tank that promotes growth and prosperity opportunities, found similar middle-class difficulties. Many families in America's struggling lower middle class—defined to include those with income between 100 percent and 250 percent of the federal poverty level, or between roughly $15,000 and $60,000, depending on family size and composition—live in economically precarious situations. Though not officially poor, these families experience limited economic security; one major setback in income could push them into poverty.[32]

THE EPIDEMIC OF THE NEW DEBTORS' PRISONS

ACCORDING TO A recent report conducted by the Brennan Center of Justice, of the approximate 1.46 million state and federal prisoners, an estimated 39 percent (approximately 576,000 people) are incarcerated for crimes that do not involve any genuine public safety concerns.[1]

Debt, historically, has been one of those crimes for which people were incarcerated. While such debtors' prisons were abolished in this country more than eighty years ago, this country is facing a new epidemic. What amounts to crimes of debt, owing money that cannot be paid back, is being invoked upon the middle-class Americans. The broad scope of infractions that a working-class citizen can commit to wind up in today's debtors' prisons has expanded in recent years. There are so many laws that do not require "intent" for a person to be found in violation, even when a genuine attempt is made to comply with them all in good faith. More and more, conduct that would be better off dealt with on an administrative or civil level, if at all, is being deemed criminal. The result is the overcriminalization of our criminal code, which is the root cause of thousands of Americans being incarcerated. Whether it is for offenses having to do with lapses in payment of child support or for traffic offenses, improprieties in banking regulations or credit, even transgressions such as fishing without a license, people are being locked up for frivolous crimes, and the taxpayers are the ones footing the bill.

You might think that a person would know when they have committed a crime, but there are countless instances where Americans have unknowingly broken the law while performing what they assume are routine everyday tasks.

THE CURIOUS CASE OF LAWRENCE LEWIS

Lawrence Lewis is an engineer who always worked hard, holding down two jobs for much of his adult life. In 2012, he was the chief engineer at a military retirement home in Washington, DC, when he was arrested after unknowingly violating the Clean Water Act while doing his job. Part of his duties included dealing with a backed-up sewage system. When it happened, he did what he been taught to do, and what had been done for years before he began working at the facility. When his staff diverted the backed-up system to a nearby storm drain that they believed emptied into the city's sewer system, Lewis was held responsible for unwittingly violating federal law. The diverted waste, in fact, flowed into a creek that fed directly into the Potomac River, a violation of the Clean Water Act. This federal statute comes with a significant fine for Lewis's employers, and for Lewis himself, a penalty of up to five years in prison.

"I couldn't believe that I was born and raised in the projects, and I worked so hard to get out that situation and build a professional career, and here I am at work getting arrested for something I had no idea was wrong,"[2] Lewis said of his arrest.

Lewis wanted to fight the charge, but since he was staring at a half-decade behind bars, his lawyer convinced him to enter a guilty plea.

"I ended up having to do that for one reason: my kids and my momma wouldn't have anywhere to live," he said. "A five-year prison sentence—they wouldn't have anywhere to live."[3]

As incomprehensible as this story sounds, it is far from unique. In fact, it happens far more often than it should, and with increasing frequency. Overcriminalization is a term that The Heritage Foundation, the American conservative think tank based in Washington, DC, describes simply as the overuse and sometimes even the misuse of the criminal law.[4] It is not a euphemism. It is real. It is a growing phenomenon, and anyone can fall prey, including people in the middle class.

Paul Larkin, a senior legal research fellow at the Heritage Foundation, is someone who has worked to shine a light on personal stories that highlight the abuse of criminal law. Larkin, who has met Lewis and talked with him, finds him to be a good and honorable man. The idea that he should have been criminally prosecuted is incomprehensible to him.[5]

As a former Department of Justice attorney and a criminal enforcement agent at the Environmental Protection Agency, Larkin believes the reason these cases are prosecuted is simple; the agents investigating such cases have supervisors telling them that if they are spending time on this, then it should end with a conviction. The prosecutors have a boss who will tell them the exact same thing. Why? Because they want to be able to go to Capitol Hill and show all the cases that they've made and to show that they need not just the money they got last year, but even more.[6]

Legal scholars anguish over regulatory growth, which sets up an often unrealistic expectation of safety while establishing an unprecedented expansion of federal criminal authority. As a result, Larkin advocates for raising public awareness as one sure way to change the course of this invasive form of crime fighting. Only when the public gets outraged about this will something happen, Larkin believes. And only then will you see prosecutors not prosecute these cases.[7] It is a sad reality that Lewis and countless other Americans continue to suffer as a result of overcriminalization. The criminal justice system should be used to protect the lives, liberty, and property of all Americans and punish truly dangerous offenders who commit crimes and deserve punishment. The system should not be used to make good, upstanding citizens look and feel like criminals.[8]

By telling his story, others might be able to avoid what he went through, but it does not solve the problem. The risk is not just humiliating an individual like Lawrence Lewis, but it is the creation of distrust of and bitterness toward our government. There seems to be enough frustration with aspects of our democracy, Washington politics in particular.

It's time to take a bold stance and honestly address these issues.

LOW CRIMES AND MISDEMEANORS

On the topic of overcriminalization, there is no better place to find examples than Capitol Hill. Traditionally, federal criminal law focused on inherently wrongful conduct: treason, murder, bank robbery, theft, counterfeiting, and the like. These days, you don't have to have your photo on display at the Post Office to be a federal criminal. This regulatory creep might be most evident in the proliferation of federal criminal statutes and the breathtaking size of the criminal code. Since the 1980s, crimes listed under Title 18 of the US Code have grown astronomically. Estimates show that Congress codifies more than fifty new criminal offenses a year. If regulatory "crimes" are included in the count, when you add all of them up, some experts believe that federal authorities can enforce in the neighborhood of 500,000 rules that could be considered a federal offense.[9] There are many volumes that cover all the different federal agencies that have the jurisdiction to enforce and interpret rules and regulations. An additional problem is that not all of the federal crimes are listed in the code. Many criminal laws are written in vague terms that fail to clearly identify what constitutes a crime, leaving Americans in the dark about whether their conduct in many cases is criminal.

According to the *PoliceOne Network*—a trusted online destination and resource for law enforcement agencies and police departments worldwide, featuring news, training, and retail information—Congress has made matters worse by giving selected federal agencies authority to establish criminal penalties for regulatory violations of what most citizens should rightly see as merely civil issues. The average citizen should know the laws of his or her country, but Americans cannot reasonably be expected to understand every potential crime when America's lawmakers themselves lack a well-defined understanding of the sprawling federal criminal code. The code should be reviewed to eliminate dated or superfluous criminal offenses so that unsuspecting citizens no longer fall victim to undeserving criminal offenses.[10]

What makes the situation even more frustrating is that for a long time there has been very little done to prevent overcriminalization through reform. However, some in Washington are aware of this injustice, and at least one influential person appears to be poised to change the status quo.

In 2013, Neil Gorsuch, the current United Stated States Supreme Court Justice, was a judge on the United States Court of Appeals for the 10th Circuit Court, when he gave a lecture for the Federalist Society in which he confronted the problem of overcriminalization, whereby criminal laws target conduct that is not inherently wrong. Using examples of obscure crimes, such as ripping off a mattress tag, Gorsuch argued that no American can possibly comprehend all the activities prohibited by federal law. Without written laws, we lack fair notice of the rules we must obey, Gorsuch said, adding that fair notice is also lacking when we have too many written laws. In other words, it's unreasonable to expect Americans to be aware of thousands of laws, much less stay on the right side of them.[11]

In 2016's *Caring Hearts Home Services v. Burwell* decision, Gorsuch had harsh words for a federal agency that forgot its own regulations and misapplied them to a home healthcare provider. Gorsuch chastised the agency, noting that it "issues literally thousands of new or revised guidance documents every single year," making it nearly impossible to know which regulations apply at any given time. He rhetorically asked: if the government itself, "the very 'expert' agency responsible for promulgating the law," cannot keep its own laws straight, how can the general public?[12]

The disconnect that exists between federal law and state law when it comes to the consequences of debt can be seen in the many shared case studies provided in this book. While federal statutes apply to everyone in this country, state and local jurisdictions are often quite disparate, with widely varying actions taken against debtors depending upon local legislation and enforcement practices. What is happening in many parts of the country when it comes to extreme penalties for fines and fees that cannot be paid is an example of overcriminalization, as Judge Gorsuch addressed in the examples above.

Our job is always in the first instance to follow Congress's directions, Gorsuch believes. But if those directions are unclear, the tie goes to the presumptively free citizen and not the prosecutor. His principle that any "tie" should go to citizens over the government shows his wariness of the vast powers possessed by prosecutors in an overcriminalized society. His tendency to view criminal laws, especially vague ones, with a healthy measure of skepticism should give opponents of overcriminalization a much-needed ally on the nation's highest court.[13]

CRIME AND PUNISHMENT

Experts like Timothy O'Toole, an attorney with Miller & Chevalier who counsels and defends clients in white collar criminal matters, contend that authority with such a broad scope will always lead to problems. He adds that once you have law enforcement people on staff, you almost consider yourself to have the mandate to go and find crime, even if the crime is previously nonexistent. O'Toole believes that US law enforcement is literally creating crime in order to justify its existence.[14]

This approach has been the cause of many citizens to become entangled in overreaching statutes, and it affects not just the poor and indigent, but the heart of the middle class and the wage earners in our country.

Federal judges, long viewed as partners in prosecution, have recently expressed concern with the type of overuse and misuse cited by O'Toole. On April 22, 2014, a federal appeals court for the Second Circuit considered exactly what constitutes insider trading, which has long been a notoriously amorphous federal crime subject to the whims of prosecutors. The appellate panel was critical of a judge for making it too easy to convict two hedge fund managers of insider trading, lending support to claims their verdict was unfair and possibly unraveling other government cases if the court ruled in favor of the defense. US Circuit Judge Barrington Parker warned that the financial sector should be assured that zealous prosecutors won't criminalize innocent actions. Sitting in the financial capital of the world, the atmosphere that you have gives precious little guidance to all the institutions and hedge funds that are trying to come up with some bright-line rule of what they can and can't do.[15]

Thus, our crippling high incarceration rates. One in every 100 adults is behind bars, and if you include those on parole or probation, the numbers show that one in every thirty-one is under some sort of correctional supervision, in no small part because of our so-called "war on drugs."[16]

According to *Time* magazine writer Fareed Zakaria, America leads the world by far in putting people in prison. The United States has 760 prisoners per 100,000 people. Compare that number to Britain with 153, Germany with 90, and Japan with 63, and it is clear that America has become a nation of criminals.[17] A primary reason for these domestic figures can only be the explosion in the number of federal laws and regulations. It is not that Americans are becoming more lawless and immoral. A recent *Wall Street Journal* bar graph showed a steady increase in the number of federal sentences in the last two decades. Whether they're crimes concerning drugs, immigration, or fraud, the rising conviction rate continues to put more people into already overcrowded prisons. The way that a growing number of Washington's laws are written, you are considered guilty even if you didn't intend to commit a crime. So if you accidentally wander into the wrong federal land, you could be prosecuted. Federal laws cover almost every aspect of life—including banking, hospitals, the Internet, your money, drugs, taxes, travel, the environment, endangered species, and far, far more.[18]

Most people have heard of the FBI, the Secret Service, and the DEA. But the truth is that many regulatory agencies have some law enforcement power.

Ilya Somin, a law professor at George Mason University, has noted that specialization is a natural result of this increasingly complex legal system with so many criminal laws. The outcome is that more than 100,000 federal officers have found a home in a variety of departments and agencies that few would suspect of needing a specialized armed capability. This list includes the National Institute of Health, the Bureau of Reclamation, the Division of Refuge Law Enforcement, the Department of Labor, the Environmental Protection Agency, and numerous offices of the Inspector General to include the Department of Education.[19]

The problems this creates is evident in numerous examples, including a case involving Kenneth Wright of Stockton, California, who was awakened early one June morning to find his house surrounded by what appeared to be a SWAT team. As if he were some fugitive from justice on the American's Ten Most Wanted List, more than a dozen federal agents, with weapons drawn and ready, were waiting for him. The officers were from the US Department of Education and were there looking for Wright's estranged wife, who had defaulted on her student loans and who was also not at the location and had not lived there for some time.

In response, the Department of Education's Inspector General's Office, which executed the search warrant, said that it does not execute search warrants for late loan payments. However, because it was an ongoing criminal investigation, of which the office conducts about thirty to thirty-five search warrants a year on issues such as bribery, fraud, and embezzlement of federal student aid funds, it refused further comment on the specifics of the Wright case.

Government at all levels routinely prohibit behavior both inside and outside the criminal code. Special interests and vocal citizens groups are good at pressuring legislators to codify just about any civil grievance with criminal legislation, which in the process only serves to divest the element of criminal intent from the equation. Bureaucrats and lawmakers are also prone to make their personal crusades part of the public agenda. Many areas are susceptible to these political whims, particularly in the environment, drug offenses, transportation, agriculture, education, and wildlife protection, and in child welfare, where status offenses, such as underage drinking, are involved.[20]

When coupled with large numbers of locally established criminal offenses, it can hardly be a surprise that people are skeptical and wary of the broad scope and reach that law enforcement has on society today. It may go a long way to help understand why some would like to see wholesale changes made to reduce the number of civil complaints that result from overcriminalization. Civil action simply fails to afford the immediate gratification derived from seeing a neighbor dragged off to jail for allowing his dog to piss on your lawn, or if one of us is unable to meet our responsibilities in a contractual agreement.

Only the most naive would believe that the states have not followed Washington's lead. Though many states don't appear to track the growth of criminal offenses officially, a Texas policy think tank has made the effort. Marc Levin of the Center for Effective Justice noted that Texas lawmakers enacted more than 1,700 criminal offenses and the state has a total of sixty-six additional felonies that are not in the Penal Code, eleven of which deal with the handling and harvesting of oysters.[21]

The argument is strong that there are so many new laws, rules, and regulations that it is all too easy to violate one of these and never know you did it. Texas retiree George Norris and his wife, Kathy, for example, were raided by federal agents who ransacked their Texas home in 2003. Because the indictment against them was initially sealed, at the time of their arrest they had not even been told why they had been targeted. Facing astronomical legal fees and a formidable foe in the federal government, George decided his only option was to plead guilty. A familiar enough story. George wound up serving nearly two years in federal prison alongside killers, rapists, and other hardened criminals. His crime? A paperwork violation related to flowers in his backyard nursery: buying, importing, and selling perfectly legal orchids. He was charged with an improper paperwork violation, but only after the government tried, and failed, to charge him with importing and selling what they thought were endangered orchids. The couple blew through their savings that could have been used to alleviate the burdens of declining health issues.[22]

Attorney Timothy O'Toole lays the blame for the explosion of US criminal law squarely at the feet of Congress and lawmakers, who need to do a better job writing narrower laws instead of trying to score points in the public relations campaign. With politicians playing both sides of the fence, it's very hard for elected lawmakers to look tough on crime while at the same time being against expanding the criminal law. Everyone wants to seem tough on crime, but I think the real problem is that nobody has been all that smart on crime.[23]

Still, it remains unlikely that legislators will roll back the number of criminal offenses or reverse the overcriminalization trend anytime soon. Lawmakers continue to pass laws so they can look "tough on crime," and law enforcement officials welcome new legislation as another tool to fight crime.[24]

DIXIELAND DISMAY

The Southern Poverty Law Center (SPLC) is a Montgomery, Alabama-based nonprofit that specializes in civil rights and public interest litigation. In 2015, this legal advocacy organization reached a settlement with Alexander City, Alabama, and its police chief to resolve a federal class-action lawsuit over the operation of a modern-day debtors' prison in which people were jailed for being unable to pay fines and court fees for traffic tickets and misdemeanors. Nearly two hundred people were jailed for nonpayment over a two-year period between September 2013 and September 2015 before the SPLC intervened, along with cocounsel Patterson Belknap Webb & Tyler, which filed suit to stop the abuse. The lawsuit described multiple violations of the US Constitution and Alabama law.

When someone appeared in municipal court for these offenses, the judge did not ask if they could pay the fines and costs. There was generally no discussion about the right to a lawyer. Nor were lawyers appointed in cases involving fines and costs. People who could not pay in full were directed to a back hallway and arrested, even when they could make a partial payment and needed time to come up with the rest. And rather than be offered community service or a payment plan, defendants were held at the city jail until someone paid the fine or until they "sat out" their time at a rate of $20 per day, or $40 if they performed jobs such as laundry, cleaning, or washing police cars. By jailing people for their inability to pay, the city violated the defendants' 14th Amendment right to due process and equal protection under the law. The arrests also violated Alabama law and the Fourth Amendment protection against unreasonable searches and seizures, as well as the Sixth Amendment, which protects individuals' right to counsel. Under terms of the settlement, the city and its insurer were ordered to pay $680,000, with the class members compensated at least $500 for each day they were illegally jailed.[25]

One plaintiff, Amanda Underwood, was jailed twice for fines she could not pay. She appeared in the Alexander City Municipal Court without counsel on her son's birthday and pleaded guilty to a traffic violation. The judge ordered her to pay a $205 fine, which she could not afford while earning $8 an hour. Unable to pay, Underwood was booked into the jail, along with five other people, including the father of her two youngest children. In June 2015, Underwood appeared in court again without counsel and was fined $250 after pleading guilty to driving without a license. Once again, unable to pay, she was immediately arrested and booked into the city jail, where she spent five days washing laundry to secure an early release.[26]

The debtors' prison practice is particularly widespread in the Deep South. In 2016, SPLC sued to stop the same kind of operation in Bogalusa, Louisiana. The city court, which has suspended its practices under a temporary agreement, was funding its operation by relying on court costs and fees. This created a conflict of interest—an incentive for the judge to find individuals guilty and to coerce payment by threatening jail. In Alabama, substantial progress has been made toward eliminating these practices. In November 2016, Montgomery Municipal Judge Lester Hayes was suspended without pay for his role in jailing the poor for nonpayment, and Perry County Circuit Judge Marvin Wiggins was censured in January 2016 for forcing the indigent to choose between jail and donating blood.[27]

Bringing to light these injustices might be the first step in correcting the problem. Holding judges accountable sends a strong message that such abuse will not be tolerated in the courts, and forcing municipalities to pay for illegally jailing people will help put an end to these unfair practices.

FISH STORY

Generally regarded as a leisurely, relaxing outdoor pastime, fishing is also a heavily regulated activity, particularly in Washington State. This regulation creates problems for law-abiding citizens who get caught up in the hunt or push the boundaries of the law in pursuit of this sport and recreation. You must know all of these regulations and abide by them all the time, with no exception or excuses. Washington State officials who enforce these regulations are notoriously zealous and heavy-handed in their investigations, charging, and enforcement, and defense attorneys understand this and must fight these kinds of cases with equal vigor. There are many different types of licenses and combinations thereof that must be properly attained and adhered to. If you want to fish with two poles, for instance, you need a two-pole endorsement on top of your normal fishing license. However, two-pole fishing is not allowed everywhere fishing is permitted. And when you fish for sturgeon, steelhead, salmon, halibut, and Puget Sound Dungeness crab, a catch record card must be used. Cards must be filled out the second after a catch has been made, and all anglers must return their catch cards by April 30. This is a requirement even if you have not caught anything or did not fish. You must further keep in mind that your fishing license can be suspended due to unpaid child support payments.[28]

It is incumbent upon the fisherman to double-check to make sure there have not been any recent emergency rules implemented. For example, as Fish & Wildlife obtains new information, such as animal fish levels in specific areas, the dates and locations of seasons may shift. If the permissible times and locations to hunt or fish change, it is important to be aware of the new regulations; otherwise, you can open yourself up to criminal prosecution. If you are contacted by law enforcement or a State agent, there is no such thing as a friendly discussion: their role is to investigate potential crimes and collect evidence.[29]

The most common criminal charge we see stemming from fishing is Unlawful Recreational Fishing in the second degree (2°). This charge can be the result of a variety of different actions or nonactions, such as failing to purchase a license and punch card, catching a fish while not having a license on your person, fishing in a closed season, or any other rule governing the method of taking fish. Unlawful Recreational Fishing in the Second Degree is a crime and is classified as a misdemeanor, which would go on your criminal record. This means it is not simply an infraction, ticket, or citation: it is a criminal charge the conviction of which will result in a mark on your criminal record. Being charged with a crime requires you to appear in court, and a conviction can result in jail, fines, probation, and more. Unlawful recreational fishing in the first degree (1°) is a more serious offense. This charge can stem from catching over double the fish limit, fishing in a fishway, certain methods of fishing (such as using spears or snares), or fishing for endangered/threatened fish, among other violations. A 1° charge is a gross misdemeanor with the risk of jail time, fines, and criminal conviction. A criminal wildlife penalty will also be imposed with a conviction if certain fish were the subject of the criminal act, such as $2,000 for a green sturgeon and $500 for wild salmon or wild steelhead.[30]

As a 19-year-old in 2011, Kyle Dewitt of Iona, Michigan, had an infant son and fiancée. At the time, he had recently lost his job at a grocery store and was out of work. One day, Dewitt decided to go fishing in a local waterway in search of dinner. To that end, he was successful, catching a fish. Unfortunately, an official from the Department of Natural Resources observed Dewitt's catch and disagreed, saying it was a smallmouth bass. Dewitt protested, but to no avail. The distinction mattered because it wasn't smallmouth season, making the catch an illegal one, which came with a $115 fine.

Dewitt was told he would be sent information in the mail telling him how to pay the fine. Weeks went by, however, and nothing happened, so Dewitt, perhaps foolishly, decided to investigate. He called to find out what had happened and learned the debt was considered unpaid and a warrant had been issued for his arrest. Further, the fine now included some additional fees, putting it at $215. Facing incarceration for nonpayment, he went to turn himself in, but a family member forked over $175 to a bail bondsman, keeping him free for the time being. A few days later, he went in front of a judge, offering to pay $100 of his fine immediately and the rest a month later—a reasonable request given that he had been unemployed for months. Not to mention that he disputed the fine in the first place, he never received a notice in the mail, and he had nonetheless turned himself in.

The judge, however, disagreed and refused to accept a partial payment. The judge said that it needed to be paid in full and even asked Dewitt if he had a credit card.[31]

To make matters worse for Dewitt, Michigan has a "pay or stay" rule, the unofficial name for a rule that basically says that if you can't pay the fine right then and there, the judge can put you in jail. It is exactly the same practice that was seen in early debtors' prisons. The "pay or stay" rule was imposed on Dewitt, and he was sentenced to three days behind bars for failing to pay the fine for catching the wrong type of fish. Dewitt didn't serve his entire sentence, thankfully. The day after his sentencing, the American Civil Liberties Union of Michigan filed an emergency petition with the court asking for his release. The petition was successful, pending a hearing of the underlying crime of snagging a smallmouth bass out of season. Dewitt avoided a jail term for his failure to pay, but that wasn't the end of his saga. As NPR reported, about a year after he got out of jail, a letter arrived in the mail. It was a bill for room and board for each day he was in jail. The new bill came to $85. The ACLU intervened, suing on behalf of Dewitt as well as four others in Michigan who were jailed because they were unable to pay misdemeanor fines.[32]

Dewitt's case is an anomaly, since he says he wasn't fishing out of season and he was never found guilty by a jury. Other cases involving the ACLU include nineteen-year-old Kristen Preston, who was unable to pay a $125 fine for underage drinking and sentenced to thirty days in jail. Dontae Smith was also nineteen when he pleaded guilty to driving on a suspended license and was ordered to pay $415 in fines. Smith was given an hour to call friends and relatives but was unable to raise the money, so Judge Joseph Longo of Ferndale, Michigan, sentenced him to forty-one days in jail. David Clark, 30, was ordered to complete a six-week parenting class and pay a $1,250 fine for spanking his girlfriend's child. Clark took the class, but he couldn't afford the fine as a part-time grocery store worker who brings home $150 a week. So Judge Randy Kalmbach of Wyandotte, Michigan, sentenced him to ninety days in jail. Dorian Bellinger, twenty-two, pleaded guilty to misdemeanor marijuana possession and couldn't afford the $425 in fees, so Judge Robert B. Brzezinski of Livonia, Michigan, sentenced him to thirteen days in jail.[33]

The ACLU is representing all five people, arguing that the cases represent a modern-day debtors' prison. Congress banned the practice of imprisoning people for unpaid debts in 1833; in the ensuing decades, most states followed with similar laws.

Elora Mukherjee, a staff attorney for the ACLU's racial justice program, believes that modern-day debtors' prisons impose devastating human costs, waste taxpayer money, and create a two-tiered justice system.[34]

While these examples may not exactly be the debtors' prisons of old, particularly in regard to the difference in the length debtors of the modern era spend behind bars, there are still many similarities. Moreover, they are clearly still being used today as a way to influence people to pay what they owe by the threat of incarceration and embarrassment.

5

GIVING OUR CHILDREN AN EDUCATION MAY COME AT AN UNEXPECTED PRICE

WANTING YOUR CHILDREN to succeed in life is a goal that all parents share, and one road to a prosperous future has always been through higher education. However, for the average middle-class family, this can be a real financial challenge even when both parents are working, sometimes more than one job, to make ends meet. If college seems to be getting more and more expensive, that's because it is. As an example, take a look at these shocking facts. In 1974, the median American family earned just under $13,000 a year. A new home could be had for $36,000, an average new car for $4,400. Attending a four-year private college cost around $2,000 a year, while a public university averaged $510 a year. To put these figures in current dollars, we're talking about a median family income of $62,000, a house for $174,000 and a sticker price of $21,300 for the car, $10,300 for the private college and $2,500 for the public one. How these costs relate today is telling when you realize that median family income has risen slightly to about $64,000, while median home prices have increased by about two-thirds, car prices have remained steady, but the real outlier is higher education. Tuition at a private college is now roughly three times as expensive as it was in 1974, costing an average of $31,000 a year; public tuition, at $9,000, has risen by nearly four times. This is a painful bill for all but the very richest. For the average American household that doesn't receive a lot of financial aid, higher education is simply out of reach.[1]

Student loan debt is increasing because government grants and support for postsecondary education have failed to keep pace with increases in college costs. Subsequently, much of the burden of paying for college has shifted from the federal and state governments to families. The government no longer carries its fair share of college costs, even though it gets a big increase in income tax revenue from college graduates.[2]

Ever-increasing tuition costs at state and private colleges and universities, coupled with the lack of adequate wage increases, make it a real struggle for many families to provide a college education for their children. With this struggle comes risk, and debt is often a consequence, the penalties for which can be more severe than just debt collection calls and a bad credit score. Young college graduates these days who receive incredibly expensive degrees also leave with an average of $35,000 in student debt,[3] and the parents are the ones who are increasingly being held responsible, putting their very freedom on the line in the process.

With college being so expensive, it might come as a shock to some parents and students when they start the financing process to learn that one form—the Free Application for Federal Student Aid (FAFSA)—may largely determine their financial fate when it comes to federal student aid. FAFSA forms are prepared annually by all current and prospective college students in the United States to determine their eligibility for student financial aid. During the process, there might be an overwhelming temptation to "fudge" the numbers on the FAFSA to get more money to help pay for your child's education. However, getting caught could spell big trouble. Filing a fraudulent claim for student financial aid is a direct violation of federal law, specifically 20 U.S.C. section 1097, which makes it a federal offense to knowingly and willfully obtain student aid funds by means of making false statements to the government. Unfortunately, federal student loan fraud is a growing trend, with more and more parents of college students being prosecuted for giving misinformation on the FAFSA. If you are convicted of this federal offense, you may have to pay a substantial fine, serve time in prison, or both.[4]

A recent decision by the United States Court of Appeals for the Ninth Circuit, *US v. Carlos Javier Ezeta* (Case No. 12-10304, May 23, 2014), illustrates how you can be charged with committing financial aid fraud.

Between 2008 and 2011, Carlos Javier Ezeta worked as a counselor and professor at the College of Southern Nevada. Motivated by his interest in helping the Hispanic community, Ezeta often assisted Spanish-speaking students in their college applications and course selections. He also helped the students obtain federal financial aid by falsifying several FAFSA applications. Based on false representations made on the forms, student aid money was dispersed to several students, including some who had not completed high school, received a GED, or passed an "ability-to-benefit" test. The US Department of Education requires that at least one of these conditions be satisfied in order for an applicant for federal student aid to be eligible. On the forms, Ezeta falsely reported that the students satisfied the education requirements and submitted the forms without the students' knowledge that they contained false information. Eight applications were generated, and six students obtained funding in the amount of $8,709. One application was intercepted before money could be dispersed, and another was never sent because the student had yet to obtain a phony certificate of high school completion. In all, the falsified documents sought financial aid amounting to over $37,000. An undercover sting operation was launched, and Ezeta eventually admitted to falsifying the applications. Although he did not personally obtain any funding, Ezeta was arrested and charged with four felony counts of financial aid fraud in violation of 20 U.S.C. section 1097(a). The Ninth Circuit Court concluded that although Ezeta did not receive any money himself, criminal liability under federal law extends to knowingly and willfully causing the funds to be disbursed to a third party by fraud, false statement, or forgery.[5]

The law is clear and the consequences severe on this statute, which prohibits anyone from knowingly and willfully embezzling, stealing, or obtaining by fraud, false statement, or forgery any funds provided for higher education purposes. If the amount of the funds provided is $200 or more, you could be charged with a felony. If you are convicted of a felony violation of financial aid fraud under federal law, you could be imprisoned for up to five years, fined a maximum of $20,000, or both. Plus, you'd have to return any aid you had received. If the funds are less than $200, you face a misdemeanor charge. A misdemeanor violation under 20 U.S.C. 1097(a) carries a sentence of not more than one year in prison, up to a $5,000 fine, or both.[6]

While this law has been in existence for decades, the prosecution for federal student loan aid is growing steadily.

Federal law also prohibits the acceptance of a loan made under false pretenses. If you are convicted of intentionally providing false information in order to obtain a federal student aid loan, you face a misdemeanor, punishable by up to one year in prison, a maximum fine of $10,000, or both. Because fraud is considered a crime of moral turpitude, a phrase used in criminal law to describe conduct that is considered contrary to community standards of justice, honesty, or good morals, a federal fraud conviction can also result in disciplinary proceedings—such as loss of a professional license (including a teaching license)—and may also lead to your deportation if you are not a US citizen.[7]

Falsifying an Application for Financial Aid is risky and foolish. In the example above, the defendant seemed to have good intentions. After all, he simply wanted to help students from the Hispanic community to pay for their college education. However, as the court pointed out, a crime committed with a "good heart" is still a crime. Additionally, the court noted the professor stood to benefit indirectly from his wrongdoing since the unlawfully obtained funding provided to his students would go to the college where he was employed.[8]

According to *Fox Business* (July 2015), one commenter in the College Confidential forums said her parents were planning to claim they were separated in an attempt to maximize their chances of financial aid. "I was definitely NOT on board with this but they refuse to listen to anything I'm saying," the student wrote.[9]

In 2014, the *Boston Globe* reported that a father of a former Harvard student pleaded guilty to charges of falsifying income information to get more than $160,000 in financial aid. He apparently filed false tax returns, which likely carries additional penalties. In another example, a college professor and counselor was charged with fraud after he allegedly falsified applications for students he said he was just trying to help. And there is the case of a mother and daughter who pleaded guilty in 2014 for making false statements to federal agents in connection with an investigation of student aid fraud. The mother reported no income for a period during which she reportedly received over $521,000 in income. So, if you're thinking of falsifying your FAFSA, just don't. And if you think you can't get caught, think again. College financial aid administrators are more skilled and experienced at detecting lies than families are at perpetrating them. In fact, about one-third of all FAFSA applications are selected for verification by the Department of Education. If yours is chosen, additional documentation will be required. An example of a red flag: the tax return shows dividends and interest on investments, but little or no assets are reported on the application.[10]

Then there are other examples such as parents who pretend they are separated. Separation is prevalent enough in society today, but in the instances where there is an informal separation, the parents must be living apart for this to be a legitimate claim, and you have to be ready to show divergent utility bills or some other form of proof that the parents are occupying two separate households. That's just one of the ways in which a lie like this can be discouraged, or uncovered.

Not telling the truth about which parent a child is living with in order to get more financial aid is another common occurrence. You can get caught easily in this lie, as well. It can slip out accidentally if a student reveals contradictory information about his or her living arrangements to a teacher or authority figure. And this is fraud. Schools are aware of this and have a compulsory responsibility to look into any instances where they suspect fraud.

A college education is expensive, and parents and students who want to avoid student loan debt may be tempted to fudge facts. But it's not worth it. If federal student loans aren't enough to cover your total student loan bill, you have other options. Private student loans are available for students and parents, but private loans (unlike federal student loans) will most likely require a credit check to determine your interest rate, and a cosigner if the borrower has a limited or nonexistent credit history. You can get a free credit report summary every month on Credit.com to see where you stand. If you have great credit, private student loans may even get you a better interest rate than Parent PLUS loans, so doing your research, improving your credit, and monitoring your progress are key.[11]

STUDENT DEBT CRISIS

Student loan debt exceeded credit card debt in 2010 and in 2011 surpassed auto loans. Over the last two decades, the average student loan debt at graduation has been growing steadily. In 1993–94, about half of bachelor's degree recipients graduated with debt, averaging a little more than $10,000. Today, more than two-thirds of college students graduate with debt, and their average debt at graduation was about $35,000.[12]

According to a February 2017 article in Forbes, it was reported that in the US, the student loan debt crisis impacts over 44 million borrowers who hold over $1.3 trillion in student loan debt.[13]

The percentage of bachelor's degree recipients graduating with excessive debt was 9.8 percent in 1993–94. Today, with regard to students who borrow to attend college, it appears that more than a quarter (27.2 percent) of them are graduating with excessive debt. The average starting salary for a bachelor's degree recipient in the humanities was about $45,000 in 2015, according to the National Association of Colleges and Employers. That compares with about $30,000 in average income for high-school graduates—or a $15,000 difference. After considering taxes, the net increase is about $9,000. Half of that ($4,500) is about 10 percent of gross income and would be enough to repay roughly $35,000 in student loans over a ten-year repayment term.[14]

Since family income has been flat since 2000, students have had to borrow more to pay for college or enroll in lower-cost colleges. That shift in enrollment, from private colleges to public colleges, and from four-year colleges to two-year ones, has also been responsible for a decline in bachelor's degree attainment among low- and moderate-income students. As a direct economic consequence of the collective student loan debt, it has been found that students who graduate with excessive debt are about 10 percent more likely to say that it caused delays in major life events, including holding off from making purchases that drive economic growth, such as buying a home. Moreover, this delay reaching other milestones like getting married and having children. They are also about 20 percent more likely to say that their debt influenced their employment plans, causing them to take a job outside their field, to work more than they desired, or to work more than one job. They are also more likely to say that their undergraduate education was not worth the financial cost. Keep in mind that students who drop out of college are four times more likely to default on their loans.[15]

Many people want to know how to avoid the pitfalls associated with the realities of trying to pay for a proper education. Educating yourself about education finances is something that is required these days because of the high cost of college and the competition for the limited resources that are available to students. If you understand the facts of what is best to do and what to avoid, you will give yourself a major advantage.

But the responsibility goes both ways, and some of the burden must fall on the institutions that are receiving certainly billions of dollars in annual tuitions.

It is therefore imperative that the federal government and the colleges and universities begin tracking the percentage of their students who are graduating with excessive debt each year. This information can then be used to improve student loan counseling. Colleges must also be given better tools to limit student borrowing. For example, college financial aid administrators must be permitted to reduce federal loan limits based on the student's enrollment status and academic major. Students who are enrolled half-time should not be able to borrow the same amount as students who are enrolled full-time. Also, our colleges must help students better understand the debt they are taking on by making the distinction between loans and grants clearer in their financial aid award letters.[16]

STUDENT DEBTORS' PRISON

In 2016, seven deputy US Marshals arrested Paul Aker in Houston, Texas, on a federal student loan from nearly thirty years before. The arrest was over a $1,500 student loan he received in 1987.[17] US Marshals Service said they made several attempts to serve Aker with a court order requesting that he appear in federal court and searched numerous known addresses. They also said that they spoke with Aker by phone and requested he appear in court.[18] When Aker didn't show up in court, a judge issued a default judgment, ordering him to pay about $2,700. Aker said he received no certified mail or notices about the outstanding debt in the past twenty-nine years, and he did not remember having had that conversation and said that he hadn't received any notification about the outstanding loan in a long time.[19]

On the day of his arrest, Aker went out to check his mail when he was approached by two marshals outside of his home. Things quickly escalated when the officers attempted to arrest him, and they discovered that Aker was armed. The marshals requested backup, and a two-hour standoff ensued before the student loan fugitive put the gun down and went outside, where he was taken into custody without further incident.[20]

After Aker was arrested, he was brought before a judge to sign a payment plan for a loan he said he made in 1987. The original loan for $1,500 now amounted to about $5,700 with interest. Aker agreed before a judge on Friday to start paying in installments of $200 a month immediately. Believe it or not, it is not uncommon for US marshals to serve summonses to people who fail to appear in court regarding outstanding federal student loans. But a warrant is only issued after someone skips a court appearance. In 2015, such warrants were issued for 1,500 people in the Houston area.[21]

Aker's experience cast much-needed light on the debtors' prison debate in general and specifically calls into question the breadth of the legal action that the government should take when someone defaults on a student loan or commits fraud in the process.

It should be duly noted that what precipitated Aker's arrest was not his failure to pay his student loan, but for ignoring a court order, something that should never be done under any circumstance, because a judge has the power to issue an arrest warrant as a result.

Joshua Cohen, a lawyer who specializes in student-loan debt, has said that borrowers cannot be arrested simply for not paying their loans. However, he cautions that if you default on your federal student loan—meaning that you miss nine consecutive monthly payments—the federal government can come after you in number of ways.[22]

DEBT BY THE NUMBERS

As implausible as it may seem for anyone to imagine winding up behind bars for not paying off a student loan, there is some precedent and case studies that reveal a threat that is very real indeed, and student debtholders have something to be worried about, even if it is not jail. Other forms of punishment are not theoretical. Take for instance the *Minnesota Daily* report that US marshals were conducting a sting to round up those in default of student loan debt.

In 2003, US marshals arrested and jailed four people in Minnesota who had defaulted on their student loans. The debtors had also failed to provide financial information at the request of federal officials. Although the debtors were not charged with a crime, they were held in jail until they agreed to turn personal financial information over to Minneapolis Federal District Court. Prosecutors planned to use that information to determine how the loans would be recouped. Before making arrests, federal prosecutors sent notices to 150 people stating that they had to send financial information to the US Attorney's Office. Of those, fifty-seven complied, while thirty had either left the state or were deceased. Individuals who ignored the statement were ordered by a court to undergo a debtor's examination. Warrants were issued for the arrest of individuals who failed to show up for the examination. Six of the ten people for whom officials obtained warrants complied. US marshals arrested the remaining four. The crackdown was dubbed Operation Anaconda Squeeze.[23] A spokesperson for the US Education Department in Washington, DC, said that the arrests, which had not been requested, were not part of a national crackdown on defaulters. US Attorney Robert Small admitted that they do not do that sort of thing very often but bottom-lined it by saying that the "threat of arrests is an effective tool."[24]

The numbers are shocking enough, with 43 million Americans saddled with outstanding student loan debt. Even more alarming is that the Federal Reserve Bank of New York shows 37 percent of debtholders are making payments and actively working to reduce their share of their student loan debt.[25]

This being the case, this leaves more than 60 percent of student-debt loan holders not making payments. What, then, are the consequences of all these debtors who are delinquent?

After the first day of missing a payment, your loan is not classified as delinquent until you take action. In the meantime, depending on your lender, you may be charged a late fee. After a month, your lender can report your missed payments to one or more of the three credit bureaus. This repeats every thirty days or until you make your payment. At day 270, and beyond, your loan goes from "delinquent" to "default." At this point, your loan becomes due in full, and immediately. Subsequently, you may see your debt garnished from your paycheck or withheld from a tax return. Many loan providers may then turn your debt over to dreaded collection agencies. As the debtor, you are responsible for paying collection fees, which can run from 18–40 percent of your student loan balance.[26]

With regard to Paul Aker, he far surpassed the 270-day mark, and after three decades of nonpayment, his creditors or collection agency had every right to litigate. The most likely way that a debtor will see the government try to collect payment is through wage garnishment.

If you are a W-2 wage earner, the government can garnish your wages with a thirty-day warning, and it does not need a lawsuit to do so. Typically, a debt collector will call a borrower's human resources department to verify they are an employee. That information is then passed along to a guarantee agency or the US Department of Education, so either one can move forward to collect on the debt via the wages. When they act promptly and request a hearing on the wage garnishment, this will temporarily stop the process and allow the borrower to work out alternate payment strategies with the loan servicer.[27]

If a person owes money but is not actively employed, another way by which the government can get back monies owed to them is Social Security garnishment. This method is more than a little unkind to people whose only source of income is the monthly Social Security checks. The government cannot look good if they are taking money away from people who are only scraping by as it is. If this were to happen, there is a measure a person can take to protect their limited income from being confiscated by Uncle Sam. For those who qualify, income-driven repayment (IDR) is a plan that allows borrowers to pay a percentage of their discretionary income toward student loan bills each month. If your discretionary income isn't above a certain level, however, your payment will be zero, until you start earning more income. If you earn at or below 150 percent of the poverty-line income, your payment will be $0.28.

Still another way through which the government can collect a debt is federal tax-refund garnishment. If you happen to have money coming back to you after filing your tax return, but still owe money from an old student loan, you will default that money back to the government.

The federal government will use the return amount to pay down the principal and interest on student loans in default, so if you are due a refund, the best thing to do might be to not file. You have up to three years to file your tax return, and in that time you could work on getting yourself out of default and then file afterward. There's no penalty to postpone filing your refund.[29]

The last resort for collecting a monetary debt is always suing the borrower. However, the government might opt for this action if you do not meet any of the above requirements (you are receiving a paycheck neither from an employer nor through Social Security, and you are not expecting money back on your taxes). That was precisely what occurred in the case we discussed earlier involving Paul Aker.

Private-loan collection operates separately from federal-loan collection. Unlike the federal government, private lenders are under no obligation to offer deferments or income-driven repayment plans. As they cannot garnish W-2 wages or Social Security payments, private lenders must pursue legal action in court. The only remedy that a private lender has is to sue you, and they are suing you under state law, and every state differs.[30]

All this being said, if you find yourself in a similar situation, the one thing you need to do above all else is to check your mailbox and be sure you pick up the telephone when it rings. That is the one sure way to avoid a possible arrest for having an outstanding student loan, whether public or private.

"It's all about power and who has control, so if a borrower ignores calls, they are taking a defensive rather than an offensive position," Cohen said.

Bottom line, if you are behind on your student loan payments, you have ways to avoid a costly court case or even an arrest. All it takes is a phone call to your lender, according to Michelle Argento of Student Loan Hero. Understanding that this first move can be worrisome, even scary, it is the best way to avoid a much harsher penalty. No matter how late your payment is, your best bet is to call your student loan servicer and admit to your mistake. The federal government offers student loan debtholders ways to return a delinquent debt (under 270 days past due) back to current. The easiest way is to pay your missed payments and any late or processing fees.[31]

There are also circumstances in which you have missed your payments due to financial hardships, such as losing a job or a medical emergency. In these cases, it is best to talk with your federal loan servicer about options, including deferment or forbearance. Getting a deferment or forbearance does not cancel your loan or the money you owe, but these options can postpone or reduce your payments based on your situation. For defaulted loans, you may qualify for a rehabilitation program in which you set up a new payment through the Department of Education. Once you have made three consecutive payments, you can additionally apply to consolidate your loans. If your loan is currently delinquent, in default, or being handled by a collections agency, you cannot be arrested for the outstanding debt. However, you should still act fast to rectify the situation and prevent future financial problems. You can create your own "get out of jail" card by contacting your lender today to potentially avoid the most extreme penalties.[32]

6
HARD WORK MAY TURN INTO A GOVERNMENT-FUNDED VACATION

MISSTEPS, NEGLIGENCE, AND outright illegality are one thing, sometimes even unavoidable, but there are some actions a person can take that have implications completely unsuspected and inappropriate to the deed. Calling in sick to go to the beach, taking office supplies for use at home, or purchasing personal items on the company credit card can all lead to termination, but did you know that they can also get you a prison sentence for fraud?

Additionally, with the local, state, and federal governments facing decreased revenues, they are seeking alternative methods to increase the flow of money to keep the tax rates as low as possible. Ironically, one way municipalities, in particular, go about raising revenue is to be aggressive with tax-related crimes and compliance.

WHO LET THE DOGS OUT?
Leave an old washing machine in your front yard, miss too many days of school, or catch a fish during the wrong season, and you could end up in jail.

Cursing in public. Playing music too loud. Rollerblading. Parking too far from the curb. Leaving old appliances in the yard. These are also some of the surprising "crimes" that CNNMoney found in databases of arrest warrants from cities an counties across the country during a months-long investigation they conducted in 2015.[1]

There is example after example of overreach by law enforcement where people are being charged with crimes that are little more than a nuisance. A small fine seems reasonable, but the following case studies illustrate just how unfair the system can be, and the clear need for considering other penalties for these "lawbreakers."

Consider 82-year-old widow Mary Root, who never thought her beloved Chihuahuas could land her in jail, but after the dogs got out of her yard a few times, she was hit with a $525 fine that she couldn't afford and a court hearing that she couldn't attend due to medical reasons. Two days later, she was behind bars and was faced with an even bigger bill of $7,000. While she was in jail, locals rallied in support of the great-grandmother. But Root isn't the only pet owner to face jail time, and it's not just a loose dog that can get people in trouble. Pets without licenses or microchips, or dogs that bark too much, are just a few of the pet-related offenses that can trigger an arrest warrant if a ticket isn't resolved.[2]

We could stop with this shocking story, but even if only to show that this is not just an isolated event and that people are frequently locked up for minor offenses, it is worth mentioning several more examples.

In Tuscaloosa, Alabama, college student Crissy Brown was driving to her job as a waitress on July 4, 2013, when a police officer pulled her over for expired car registration tags. The officer looked her up in the system and found that there was a warrant out for her arrest. He then promptly put her in handcuffs and took her to jail. It turned out that the warrant stemmed from a prior unpaid ticket, also for her expired registration. After receiving that initial ticket, Brown had spoken with a judge and was given a second hearing. But when that hearing came around, she didn't have the money and

feared that if she showed up to court again, she would be thrown in jail. So she didn't go.[3]

What happened next may not come as a big surprise. A warrant for the woman's arrest was issued. Brown disputes that she was ever given the option of paying the fine in increments over time rather than all at once, but they made an example out of her and treated her as they would any fugitive from justice.

The incarceration itself was brief—she was quickly bailed out by her parents—but the consequences she suffered is where the real injustice lay: her car was impounded, costing her additional $150 in fees; she also lost her job for missing work while incarcerated.

Then there is the case of Frank Ward, a senior citizen from Baytown, Texas, who used his Social Security money to keep his grandsons out of jail for missing school. Authorities never considered that the reason they missed so many days of school was that a family situation forced many of their absences, including ten in the previous two years alone. When they were living twenty miles from their school, with no bus route close to their house, being tardy and occasionally not making it to school was inevitable.

Ward said his grandsons couldn't get to school because of a bad family situation that resulted in more than a dozen moves in two years. That ultimately left the boys as much as twenty miles from school, making options like the bus often unavailable. Ward didn't find out about the citations until his seventeen-year-old grandson ended up in jail for failing to pay fines that had ballooned to $950. The other grandson owed $360 but had not been arrested. Ward has since used more than $1,300 of his Social Security benefits to clear both boys' warrants and is still angry that they ended up in criminal court in the first place.[4]

Texas was one of only two states to consider truancy a crime. Under the law, Texas Education Code 25.0951, it was mandated that schools file charges against students with more than ten unexcused absences over six months, or three in four weeks.[5] In 2013, the Lone Star State prosecuted over

115,000 kids for missing school, Class C misdemeanors. The result was that seventeen-year-old students could get locked up with adult criminals guilty of everything from burglary to violent crimes, all the while missing more school. Some kids found themselves expelled because of these court-mandated absences, a tragic irony for a truancy system meant to scare teens into taking school seriously. Even though they were minors, Texas students facing truancy charges had to appear in adult criminal court and faced hefty fines of up to $500. Once found guilty of the crime, students were offered the choice to pay the fines in full or earn a credit of up to $300 for every day spent in jail. For those who couldn't afford the fine, plus the additional court costs, arrest warrants would be issued for failing to pay, and these students found themselves in a modern-day version of debtors' prison.[6]

This section wouldn't be complete without the case of Diane Tran being mentioned. It speaks to the notion that even if laws are changed, it is another matter changing hearts and minds, even those of a judge. Tran was seventeen, an honors student, taking college classes and working part-time to help support her younger sister after their parents left them. This young woman was thrown into jail for excessive truancy. How long she remained there is not the issue here, but what the judge said when issuing a warning to her. "If you let one run loose, what are you gonna do with the rest of 'em? A little stay in the jail for one night is not a death sentence,"[7] Judge Lanny Moriarty said, serving justice like a waiter in a diner filing an empty coffee cup.

Then there is the unlikely case of a Dallas County twelve-year-old girl, Peyton Walker, who was taken out of her 7th-grade class by police, hand-cuffed, and arrested for excessive unexcused absences. No consideration was made for the illness of the girl's mother, which caused her to suffer from severe anxiety and headaches. This made her miss school, as well as miss a court appearance to answer to truancy charges.

If it were the only such example, it might be excused as a bad case of over-sight. But how much was learned from the arrest of the twelve-year-old when several years later, it was still not made right? The girl's disabled mother still

had over $2,000 in pending fines, an amount that barred the teen from getting her driver's license until it is paid.[8]

Outrage over the former laws poured in from nonprofit groups, state legislators, and even the chief justice of the Texas Supreme Court, until finally in 2015, Texas Governor Greg Abbott signed a bill into law that decriminalized skipping school, making truancy a civil offense. As a consequence, truant students will face escalating fines instead of jail time, and schools have been empowered to impose a "behavior improvement plan" on students as an alternative to court appearances, putting kids into community service and counseling programs instead of prison cells. Also, schools will no longer be able to refer students to court if their absences are the result of pregnancy, homelessness, or being the primary breadwinner for their family. The Texas law also allowed for the expungement of past convictions, providing thousands of convicted students a welcome, clean slate. Despite Gov. Abbott making the bill official, it is unclear what will become of the massive amount of money currently owed in truancy fines. With groups claiming that truancy laws were being used to force students with disabilities out of school, this issue is far from over.[9]

TO ERR IS HUMAN

When a summons or a fine replaces arrest as the penalty for certain crimes, it seems that it only adds another step before ultimately putting someone into a modern-day debtors' prison. If someone cannot pay the fine, or if they miss a court appearance, an arrest will follow.

In Manhattan recently, relief was given for people who relieve themselves in public. Urinating in public, as well as other minor offenses, such as littering, were no longer an arrestable offense of as March 2016.

Under the terms of the initiative, low-level criminal offenses such as public consumption of alcohol and taking up two seats on the subway for offenders won't result in arrests or prosecutions, just summonses. In order to downplay the significance of this new ordinance, officials stated that the offenses being "downgraded" typically did not result in arrests anyway, unless officers found out that the offenders had an open warrant, or did not have an ID, in which case they were required to make an arrest. Under the reforms, low-level criminal offenders with open warrants would still be taken into custody and then to court, but they would not have to deal with a new criminal case, just a summons. Offenders who simply didn't have an ID, meanwhile, were to be given time to call someone to the station house with a photo ID before being arrested.[10]

Officials touted the program as a way to allow the police, as well as the judiciary, to concentrate on more serious crimes, with estimates that the move resulted in the diversion of 10,000 cases annually that would otherwise have to go through Manhattan Criminal Court.[11]

Once more, these kinds of changes, while doing exactly what they were intended to do, can also lead to a problem that may not have been fully considered. When infractions become a source of revenue, regardless of what other attributes they have, can people with limited income still have their freedom threatened when they find themselves unable to pay their summons or fine? The answer is a resounding "yes."

A Daily News analysis published in 2014 showed the overwhelming majority of summonses issued by the NYPD citywide were to black and Latino men. Roughly 81 percent of the 7.3 million people hit with quality-of-life violations between 2001 and 2013 were black or Hispanic. Alcohol consumption was the most common offense.[12]

Not everybody was happy, as is so often the case with any decision made in the public's interest. Some didn't think the law went far enough, including City Council Speaker Melissa Mark-Viverito, who made a bid to decriminalize the same offenses that would now not be prosecuted. The agencies pushed back with the release of a statement noting that "Should an NYPD officer determine that the public is best served by arresting an individual who would ordinarily receive a criminal summons, that officer will still have the option to do so."[13]

Robert Gangi, cofounder of PROP (Police Reform Organizing Project), an advocacy group that's long called for reforms to the summons system, was unimpressed with the changes, calling them a tweaking at best, not a major change.[14]

Gangi is a recognized expert on criminal justice and law enforcement issues with a particular focus on police and prison reform. He is dedicated to the rights of vulnerable people caught up in the criminal justice system.

While you can't please everybody with any law, it shows that changes can be made for the better, and that more progress can be made.

SHOW ME THE MONEY

While arrests for a minor offense can be avoided, the same offense can still land you in jail. And while such a statement may sound incongruous, it is not doublespeak. Government agencies across the country are increasingly hiring private debt collectors to go after millions of Americans over unpaid taxes, as well as other monies owed to them by citizens, including outstanding parking tickets and even road tolls. For any administration, this is an effective way to put some money back into the coffers, but by outsourcing collections, they are giving these private companies license to charge debtors whatever they want, while offering their services to government agencies at no cost. Their profits are made directly from the fees passed on to the debtors. At the same time, state legislators have passed laws permitting these collection agencies to charge debtors steep fees. In Florida, for example, fees can be as high as 40 percent on top of the total bill, which includes not only what debtors already owe, but interest and government penalties, as well. In Texas, fees can reach 30 percent. And in cases of unpaid toll violations, flat fees can effectively amount to more than 100 percent. As a result, small unpaid tolls can easily balloon into hundreds of dollars, once government penalties and collection fees are tacked on.[15]

Various strong-arm techniques by collection agencies are permitted, including threatening debtors with the suspension of their driver's license, garnishment of their wages, foreclosure, and arrest to get them to pay up. And it's all legal.

Linebarger Goggan Blair & Sampson, a Texas-based law firm, is a big player in this industry. The firm promotes themselves as a "profession collection services by licensed attorneys." They have worked for small-town school districts, the city of New York, and, at one point, the largest tax collector in the country: the Internal Revenue Service. Linebarger works for 2,300 clients nationwide and collects $1 billion for its clients each year.[16]

Is this the best way to go about collecting funds for vital services? The fees get collected to the benefit of municipal, state, and even federal coffers, and law firms like Linebarger make a profit, but is that all there is to it? Do the benefits outweigh the drawbacks?

Government agencies sometimes hire Linebarger to hunt down decades-old debt, while some turn over unpaid bills to collections mere months after consumers have incurred them. Still others provide the firm with inaccurate information, leading it to pursue the wrong person entirely. These agencies can issue the arrest warrants, foreclosure lawsuits, and other means of pressure that Linebarger cites in its letters to debtors.[17]

These are serious problems that should not be overlooked. The best way to illustrate the problems that are inherent in this type of debt collection system is through specific examples.

In 2013, Oklahoma restaurant manager Mike Knight was billed $112,000 over the sales tax for a business he used to own. Less than half of the bill was for taxes he already paid in 2004. The rest was for government interest azebarger's collection fees. But his bank no longer had his proof of payment, so it took months and $800 in legal fees to convince Linebarger he had paid his taxes. Knight has said he was guilty until proven innocent, and that he didn't know if he would be going to jail, or if his house would be taken.[18]

He had to live every day with this cloud of uncertainty handing over his head. Even after it was resolved, there was little satisfaction. Certainly, there was no apology, and even after the mistake was recognized, with the

Oklahoma Tax Commission "working to improve its system to make it easier for taxpayers to dispute bills," that is far from a guarantee.

Then there is Jane Lopez, who spent a year battling Linebarger over a $6,200 bill for a time when Chicago firefighters had put out a fire at a property she no longer owned. What made the situation even more frustrating was that it turned out the fire hadn't even occurred at her building; it was at a place next door. Convinced it was a scam, she warned others about the firm on RipoffReport.com. And when she learned the firm was legitimate, she was even more scared. She became a nervous wreck, fearful that she would be sued. After Lopez sent Linebarger a photo of the property, she says she never heard from them again, but she is still on edge about what they might do next. There is also the story of an out-of-town driver who mistakenly failed to pay $7.50 in tolls on a Texas highway and found his penalty fee quickly mounting to $157.50. The driver owed the original toll amount, plus $66 in administrative fees, while Linebarger added $84 for itself.[19]

The Harris County Toll Road Authority in Texas has said that it uses the funds collected by Linebarger to help keep Houston's toll roads drivable and safe. For their part, Linebarger maintained that its fees are reasonable and dependent upon the kind of debt and how hard it is to collect. By collecting these fees directly from the debtor and not charging the municipalities, Linebarger said this keeps taxpayers from subsidizing its collection costs. This practice is different from that of a consumer creditor like a bank, which typically has to pay for its collection costs out of the money recovered from debtors.[20]

In CNNMoney's investigation and accompanying article, "The Secret World of Government Debt Collection," they exposed a secret that is no secret to a lot of people. And they named names in the process. They looked into the practices of a law firm that worked for the government as a collection agency. Besides the individual horror stories of some of the people involved, what the report showed was that the law firm hired to collect the debt was wholly unaccountable and could do practically whatever they wanted without recourse. In essence, this private law firm operated above the law.

Thanks to legal exemptions, government collectors usually don't have to follow the main federal law that regulates the debt collection industry. State consumer protection laws often don't apply, either. And when debtors have challenged Linebarger's actions in court, the firm has gone so far as to argue it has immunity because it is an extension of the government.[21]

This is a frightful proposition. It leaves a private citizen, who is already in debt trouble, with no protection, and going up against not just the government, but a private company that is acting as a proxy for the government, with all the overreach protections inherent in the bureaucracy. Even more alarming is that many private firms are given these privileges as collection agencies for the state.

Like most matters, the devil is in the details, and some of the methods used in pursuit of debt collection for the government have been called into question. While Linebarger has maintained that consumers typically receive at least one notice, and sometimes multiple notices, from the government before a debt ends up in collections, many people dispute this claim. Some have said that the government never notified them, and Linebarger's threatening letters and phone calls were the first they had heard of their debt. Complaints have been filed in the public domain as well as with the BBB, so there is ample proof that there is a disconnect there, and a problem that needs to be addressed. Numerous people did not believe that Linebarger was legit and dismissed their phone calls as a scam to defraud them. On occasion, mistakes were made, with subjects wrongfully named as debtors. In all these cases, the threat of being deprived of individual freedoms, which included being incarcerated, was a real possibility if the situation was not rectified.

Despite a class-action lawsuit challenging the fees Linebarger charged under a contract with the city of New Orleans, whereby the Louisiana Supreme Court ruled that the firm's 30 percent fees were unconstitutional, the firm got hired to collect money from people who owed money to the government, and they always received a set amount for their effort—even when they were able to negotiate down the outstanding amount a consumer owed in back taxes.[22] It does not sound right, and Linebarger doesn't appear to have much sympathy in the process. In a response to a man who accrued a $287 debt over an original $1.25 toll charge, a partner of the firm replied, "While we understand that this is frustrating to some debtors, they can avoid all fees by doing what the vast majority of Americans do—pay their tolls when they're due instead of allowing them to go delinquent."[23]

One of the most profound examples of heartlessness can be seen in the case of a New York City mother, Laverne Dobbinson, who received a bill from Linebarger in 2012 charging her recently deceased son $710 for the damage to the city police car that killed him. The outrage and horror over this injustice was incomprehensible to the Dobbinson family and everyone who read about the incident. The City of New York did not offer an official comment, but at the time, the City acknowledged to one journalist that the letter had been sent in error. Even when the mistake is clearly on the part of one of Linebarger's clients, those who end up in the law firm's crosshairs seem to have little recourse. Going up against the IRS is a no-win situation. Unlike consumer debt, where you are afforded a number of protections by federal and state statutes, as well as the ability to seek justice through the state A.G.'s office and agencies like the Consumer Financial Protection Bureau.

The main federal law regulating debt collectors is the Fair Debt Collection Practices Act, which prohibits collectors from charging any fee that wasn't already agreed to in a contract or permitted by state law. Collectors also aren't allowed to make false threats of arrest, and they are required to provide proof that a debt was incurred if the debtor requests it. Federal consumer protection rules rarely apply to the government debts Linebarger collects, however, because they usually aren't considered "consumer debts." Speeding tickets and property taxes, for example, aren't considered a service or product that has been purchased, as is an unpaid water bill.[24]

Despite decades of scandals and bad press surrounding the firm and its partners, including allegations of bribery to influence lawmakers, Linebarger continues to land lucrative government contracts, wield widespread political influence, and rake in new million-dollar contracts. But even if all of the politicians and government agencies end their relationships with Linebarger, there are still many other private collectors that would be happy to take its place. What is really needed, consumer advocates say, is an end to the special treatment given to government debt collectors. Until then, millions of Americans are left facing ominous threats and steep fees each year.[25]

THE TAXMAN COMETH

"The hardest thing in the world to understand is the income tax," said Albert Einstein, regarded as one of the most brilliant minds in our time. The physicist and genius who gave us the theory of relativity had trouble deciphering the modern tax code, which has also been likened to the horror movie *The Blob* for its amorphous shape and the fact that it just keeps getting bigger and bigger the more you try to kill it. Notoriously confusing, and changing all the time, it makes you wonder if anybody truly understands it, or if they are just pretending they do.

Tax problems are nothing new, and individual stories about the horrors of getting caught up in the gears of this system are far too numerous to report. Several examples will suffice, and those involving people considered in the middle class are the one that we will focus on here. These are the cases that involve average, hardworking Americans and the owners of small businesses, all of whom are trying to do the right thing and pay their fair share of taxes. When a mistake is made on either side, by the taxpayer, the tax payer's accountant, or the IRS, it frequently does not matter. The problem usually takes a very long time to resolve, and when it does, it is at a huge cost to the taxpayer, who might have lost everything in the fight for exoneration.

Probably one of the most well-known recent cases involved a Queensbury, New York, man, David Monsour. In 2012, he was charged with six felony charges of criminal tax fraud and offering a false instrument for filing based on allegations he evaded about $70,000 in taxes on $950,000 in income between 2006 and 2009.[26] William Comiskey, Monsour's lawyer, called the case troubling and perplexing because the state Department of Taxation & Finance didn't give his client a chance to explain his situation before having him charged. If investigators had done so, they would have learned Monsour had done nothing wrong. Comiskey said the state had incorrectly calculated what Monsour owed. Basically, income from sales of property, proceeds from mortgages, and other income that was exempt were counted against Monsour's tax liability. The Warren County District Attorney's Office reviewed the information provided by Comiskey and presented it to the Tax Department, and the prosecutor's office concurred with Comiskey's finding.[27]

Because Monsour lacked any criminal intent, since his taxes were prepared by a professional accountant whom some might describe in this case as aggressive in his filing practice, it was easy for Warren County Judge John Hall to have the six-count indictment against the man dismissed. The mistake was not Monsour's, and it was not as big of a mistake as it was first thought. Monsour agreed to pay $7,408 to the state for unpaid taxes. Although Comiskey commented that whether he owed that money or not was questionable, Mansour decided to pay it as a way to bring about a swift resolution to the ordeal.

While the charges against Monsour were dismissed, the crimes were reported in the media, and as a result, his reputation was ruined and his businesses crippled. This kind of thing happens more than you think, and many working people and business owners in this country may not be as fortunate as Dave Monsour.[28]

PLEASE TIP YOUR WAITRESSES AND BARTENDERS

Many people who work in the service industry rely on tips, not just for extra money, but as part of their salary. In cash businesses, it's tempting for middle- and low-income earners in these various fields to underreport the tips they earn. As unlikely as it might be to get caught, it can happen, and it does happen, and not only are the employees who cheat on their taxes held accountable, but so, too, might the employer.

Avoiding trouble with the IRS if you work in the service industry seems straightforward enough: declare all your tips as income. But what are the rules? What does that law say?

State income tax law varies, and different states impose varying degrees of penalties on salons and stylists for not properly recording their tips. Some states have actually gone after salons and stylists for not claiming their tips. There have been examples in Texas and South Carolina where salons are receiving enormous fines as well as losing their business licenses. The only way to know for sure is to check your state's tax code and enforcement policies.[29]

Federal law is more uniform, and, whether given in cash or credit, tips amounting to more than $20 per month are considered taxable income. As taxable income, tips are subject to the federal income tax. This has always been the law, and recently the IRS has been increasingly trying to close the tip income loophole, which has been growing significantly larger with time. This added scrutiny has led to a sharp uptick in audits for service industry employees. If an audit shows you have been underreporting your tips, you can be subject to outrageously high fines with interest.[30]

If the taxman uncovers that you are underreporting your tips, you can expect a severe financial penalty, a fine with interest, and we know what can happen if those fines go unpaid. Regardless of the industry (hairdresser, waitress, bartender, bellhop, or any other service industry job), you are putting yourself at risk by not declaring your tips as taxable income.

If you earn tips, you are responsible for paying not only income, but also Social Security and Medicare, tax on the tip money you receive. There are a few things to keep in mind if you earn tips and other cash income. First, the IRS requires you to report your total monthly tips to your employer by the

10th of the following month. If your employer doesn't have a process for reporting tip income, you can use Form 4070. If you fail to report your tips to your employer, the IRS can impose a penalty equal to 50 percent of the Social Security and Medicare tax you fail to pay. The IRS requires your employer to withhold enough money from your wages; however, the amount withheld is based on the total sum of your wages plus the tip income you report, even if you receive the tips directly from the customer in cash. Your employer will pass along your figures to the IRS and take money out of your wages to cover tip withholding. If you don't earn at least $20 in tips during the month, you don't have to report the tips to your employer. If you work at more than one job, apply the $20 limit to each one. However, you still need to include these tips in taxable income when you prepare your income tax return.[31]

If you didn't earn enough in wages and tips that your employer pays to you directly to cover your tax withholding, the W-2 would show how much tax you still owe. If the amount you underpay is significant, you may be liable for estimated tax penalties after you file your tax return. Fill out Form 4137 for any unreported tip income, which will cover the months when your tips total less than $20, as well as the value of any noncash tips you receive. Add this amount to your reported tips and wages to get your total taxable income. Form 4137 includes instructions for calculating the Social Security and Medicare tax you must pay on your unreported tip income. The IRS assumes that restaurants and similar businesses generate tips equal to at least 8 percent of sales. If a business only reports annual tips equal to 6 percent of sales, for example, the IRS requires the employer to allocate the remaining 2 percent of sales among employees, and you must include your share in taxable income.[32]

WHAT EXACTLY IS TAX FRAUD?

While filing a tax return is referred to as "voluntary compliance," individuals are expected to know the laws and must file when required to do so. Tax fraud occurs when individuals working and earning income knowingly and intentionally fail to file their income tax return, or falsify information on a tax return. Failing to state the correct amount of earned income, overstating deductions and exemptions, and falsifying documents are all possible elements of tax fraud and are punishable in both criminal and civil jurisdictions. The process of concealing or transferring income and reporting personal expenses as business expenses are also examples of tax fraud and are actual violations of the law.[33]

IRS Criminal Investigations (CI) is the law enforcement branch of the IRS. CIs are conducted for American taxpayers who willfully, knowingly, and intentionally violate their legal requirement to file their tax returns and pay their taxes every year. The General Tax Fraud Program is the largest Criminal Investigation enforcement program within the IRS. The General Tax Fraud Program encompasses CIs ranging from tax evasion to money laundering crimes. CIs are conducted for individuals and businesses across all industries and locations in the country. Of the CIs completed, General Tax Fraud cases require the most substantial amount of CIs' resources and investigation efforts to ensure taxpayer compliance with IRS rules and regulations.[34]

Criminal investigations look at the stated amount of income, place, and duration of stated employment, and payment of excise taxes. They can charge individuals with a number of crimes, all of which fall into four major crime categories: Legal Source Tax Crimes; Illegal Source Financial Crimes; Narcotics-Related Financial Crimes; and Counterterrorism Financing. Many of the crimes within the jurisdiction of CI have criminal and civil liabilities attached. Crimes that individuals can be charged with include, but are not limited to: Tax Evasion; Attempt to Defeat Tax; Tax Evasion Avoidance; Additional Tax Due; Willful Failure to Pay; Willful Failure to Keep Records; and Fraudulent Statement to Employer. If an individual is caught cheating on his or her taxes, there are civil and possible criminal consequences. Civil penalties include assessing interest on taxes due for the entire period of time for which they are outstanding, and unlike criminal penalties, civil penalties can accrue indefinitely.[35]

Individuals who underreport their income by 25 percent or more are within the fraud provisions of the IRS rules, and as such, the IRS will be able to go back for six years (as opposed to the normal three-year statute of limitations) to charge the individual with an underpayment tax penalty. If the IRS substantiates a claim of willful intent to evade paying taxes, they could go back as far as they wish, without any limitation, and assess penalties, fines, and interest on all unpaid taxes from the beginning of the taxpayer's adult life. Individual taxpayers being prosecuted for tax evasion penalties and crimes should immediately seek the assistance of an experienced tax attorney who can help them understand the severity of the charges and available options. Often, an agreement can be reached out of court that allows the individual to pay fines and penalties in lieu of going to jail. If attempts to reach a plea bargain fail and the case goes to trial, there is a substantial likelihood that those charged with significant tax crimes will end up serving jail time. Federal Sentencing Guidelines establish the length of time for convicted tax criminals, but many in-court and out-of-court factors may also play a part in determining the punishment upon conviction.[36]

Consequences for not filing a tax return can include both criminal and civil penalties. Criminal Consequences: criminal charges may be brought against an individual within six years of the date by which the tax return should have been filed. Additionally, nonfilers can be fined up to $25,000 per year and may also be put in prison for one year for each year of nonfiling. Civil Consequences: civil penalties include assessing the interest of taxes due for the entire period for which they are outstanding. While criminal consequences are limited to six years, civil penalties can accrue indefinitely.[37]

7

SLOW DOWN OR ELSE...

EVERYONE HATES TICKETS, but for some people, they are more than just a nuisance and a minor hit to the wallet. Thousands of Americans have been sent to jail not for committing a crime, but because they cannot afford to pay for traffic fines, court fees, and penalties that come with them.

While some infractions are considered misdemeanor criminal offenses, in some cities and states failing to pay fines can trigger an arrest warrant. In Ferguson, Missouri, for example, a 2015 Department of Justice report found that the city had almost as many active arrest warrants as it had residents and that many of these warrants stemmed from minor offenses, such as traffic-related tickets.[1]

Some believe the warrants are a last ditch effort to get people to settle their debts, but they happen, and it doesn't matter who you are. Here's how they can happen: Let's say you get a speeding ticket. Typically, you're given a certain amount of time to pay the fine or challenge it in court.[2] But if you don't show up to the hearing or pay the fine, some courts will issue a warrant for your arrest, placing you on the same list as alleged rapists, thieves, and escaped prisoners.

THE ROAD TO DEBTORS' PRISON

Many of the middle class are living paycheck to paycheck and struggling to keep their heads above water. Perhaps you recently lost your job due to your company closing, downsizing, or moving out of state, or maybe you're working two part-time jobs until you can find a good-paying position in your field of choice. The fear many working people have that an unexpected expense can come along that can put them in over their heads is a real one. Imagine running late to work one morning, and you are speeding because you can't afford to be late again. You get pulled over and get a $200 ticket for speeding. You're barely getting by, and paying this ticket would mean not paying for the kids' daycare or your utility bill that month. As a result, you don't pay the fine or go to court because you can't afford to take the day off from work. Now, there is a bench warrant issued, and the court sends your information to the DMV to suspend your license. Because of this, your license is suspended, but you still need to go to work, so you continue to drive because public transportation won't get you there. Then the worst thing happens, and you get pulled over again or get into an accident. You are now charged with a crime: operating on a suspended license. At this point, the only way to avoid jail is to pay the original $200 fine, plus penalties, court costs, warrant fees, and any new fines from the new charge. It's just a matter of time before you are imprisoned for nonpayment, and likely lose your job, allowing you no way to pay this debt or any of your other family bills.

Such consequences are inevitable. There are 222 million licensed drivers in America today.[3] As Americans, we pay more than six billion dollars in fines for traffic offenses each year.[4] A literal cash cow for municipal and state governments nationwide. This is one reason why politicians throughout America can avoid doing the unthinkable: raising taxes.

Instead, they stabilize taxes by increasing revenue in other areas.

A study of municipal, county, and state budgets nationwide has shown that governments faced with reduced revenues rely quite a bit on traffic offenses to pay for their expenses, to the point that they budget with the expectation that motorists will break the law.

Municipalities use a ticket quota system to force officers to write more tickets or dangle the opportunity for overtime to officers to go out and raise revenue. And state governments budget with the expectation that officers will write x number of tickets. And whether it is called "traffic-calming measures," "accident reduction," or something else, it is all for the same purpose: taxation by citation. Whatever you label it, it all comes at a cost to the working people in America. When the ordinary government revenue goes down, significant increases are seen in the issuance of traffic tickets.

The constitutionality of a ticket quota system is controversial and much debated, but it happens everywhere, and there seemingly is not a lot that can be done about it.

For instance, in 2006, the Mayor of Nashville, Tennessee, proposed a budget with a 33 percent revenue increase from traffic tickets.[5] Mayors, town councils, city managers, and others can't depend on the Department of Public Works to raise revenue, so they look to the police departments. Ironically enough, if you travel the country during an election year, you will hear all the same rhetoric from politicians. Keep taxes down and make the community safe. If the all those promises came true and we all were safe drivers, the system would go broke. In fact, in small town America, the revenue from traffic tickets accounts for more than 60 percent of the town's budget. In Ferguson, Missouri, for example, the reliance on revenue from traffic fines and court fees has become so great that they have seen an 80 percent increase in court revenue from 2011 to 2013. For a St. Louis suburb of about 21,000 residents, the ticket revenue equaled more than 2.5 million dollars in 2014. Most drivers are completely unaware of this trend of skyrocketing tickets because it is so recent.[6]

The hottest trend to generate revenue is the installation of red light cameras. Originally, these cameras were pitched as safety devices to make intersections safer and act as a deterrent. Now, communities rely on the revenue generated from the cameras to balance budgets. In 2012, motorists in the State of Florida paid over 100 million dollars for red light camera offenses. The question remains, are the roads safer or are the coffers of the state and local governments just larger? A study conducted in St. Petersburg, Florida, showed a decrease in side-impact collisions but an increase in rear-end collisions caused by people stopping short at intersections with red light cameras to avoid the fines. As of 2013, twenty-four states and the District of Columbia had installed red light cameras, and the average ticket was approximately $100 with the highest penalty in California at a whopping $490. These automated traffic cameras raise an enormous amount of cash for communities. In the District of Columbia, speeding and traffic light cameras raised $50.9 million in 2010, and as they installed more cameras, it increased to $84.9 million in just two years. In Providence, Rhode Island, a city with no viable mass transit system, the coffers took in $137,092 in 2014 for fines from red light cameras to predicting revenue from the same source to be over $1.2 million in expected income in 2018. There has been roughly an 89 percent increase in four years.[7]

TICKET TO RIDE

Now that we showed you how the government uses these back-door tax methods to raise revenue, how do the communities assure the revenue keeps flowing? One of the more tried-and-true methods is ticket quotas. Ticket quotas are the requirement by a police department that officers must issue a minimum number of tickets for moving violations or even making arrests. Police chiefs throughout the country consistently deny they exist, but evidence suggests otherwise. Some states have gone as far as Florida and have made quotas illegal, as stated in Title XXIII Motor Vehicles 316.640: "An agency of the state as described in subparagraph 1 is prohibited from establishing a traffic citation quota."[8]

Regardless, communities are addicted to the ticket revenue like a drug. They either fly in the face of laws banning such quotas or find ways around them with performance-based bonuses. For instance, look at Waldo, Florida, a small town north of Ocala with a population of approximately 1,000 people. In 2014, the town had one red light and seven police officers. The police chief, in violation of the law, ordered every officer to write twelve tickets per twelve-hour shift or be disciplined. In 2013, officers in that town brought in $400,000 in revenue, equaling a third of the town's total revenue. After repeated ticket quotas were brought to light in violation of state law, the town voted to disband the police department and rely solely on the sheriff's department for law enforcement.[9]

In Michigan, a twenty-five-year police veteran sued his department, alleging he was forced into early retirement because he refused to meet ticket quotas to raise revenue. The department settled with the officer for $280,000. Similarly, in 2013, government officials were forced to conduct an investigation on ticket quotas in East Orange, NJ. New Jersey is another state that has outlawed quotas. However, the administration in New Jersey denies any quotas exist, saying it is the job of the officer to write tickets, and if they don't perform their jobs appropriately, they will be disciplined.[10]

Departments are also crafting creative ways to get around calling a ticket quota exactly what it is. Therefore, departments have performance-based incentives for writing tickets instead. For instance, in Atlanta, police fund pay raises through ticket revenue. If the officers want to ensure they get a raise, they had better write more tickets and show up in court to defend them. This system was spelled out in an email to officers from their chief, saying that ticket revenue is tied to future pay raises.[11] If police know their raises are tied to ticket revenue, they will be more inclined to write more tickets for minor offenses that may have been overlooked in the past.

There are certainly many departments throughout the country that tie overtime to officers who write tickets. Departments routinely have programs where an officer is given, for example, four hours of overtime to write ten tickets. An officer who writes ten tickets in the first hour can go home and collect the remaining three hours of overtime while sitting in the comfort of his or her own home.[12]

Now that we have discussed how governments across the country are using tickets, a supposed deterrent to illegal behavior, as a designated source of revenue for city budgets, how does all this relate to the middle class?

WORKING-CLASS DOGS

As pointed out in an earlier chapter, when it comes to the middle class, some people think it akin to running in place, working harder but not getting anywhere, and certainly not improving your economic status. In reality, being in the middle class is not something that is static. It changes. A person can move up in economic status, just as a person can move down. Anything that threatens a person's ability to get and keep a job can plunge that person and their family beneath the middle class with no hope of getting back. We travel to work every day to make ends meet and support our families. Hitting people with unexpected expenses and even the threat of taking away their ability to drive legally strikes at the heart of the American Dream.

As we have seen in history, debtors were by far the largest element in the 18th-century prison population. Today, over 20 percent of our country's prison population is being incarcerated for financial reasons.[13] Prison for debt is a trend that continues to rise, ensnaring the middle class. Just as a person could be sent to debtors' prison in Victorian England for owing the smallest amount of money, that is something that is happening today in this country on a regular basis. Most people today are unaware that they are at risk of being jailed for failure to pay court costs and other penalties and fines for something as benign as a traffic ticket, because that was not the case even a few years ago.

In Victorian England, like now, being jailed for any length of time was a detriment not just to the defendant, but his entire family. Today, fines get increased, and if the offender is unable to drive and work, perhaps even losing a job as a result of incarceration, this only serves to pull the family out of the middle class and into poverty.

Over the past few years, the high national rate of unemployment has hit all Americans, and government fiscal shortfalls that followed the housing crash have increased the use of debtors' prisons, as states look for ways to replenish their coffers. Cash-strapped cities and states increasingly are trying to tap a previously overlooked pot of money—uncollected fines, fees, and other costs imposed by civil and criminal courts—in order to help them balance their books. And when people don't pay these court-ordered debts, some local officials have not been shy about tossing them in jail, leading to the creation of modern-day "debtors' prisons."

According to Roopal Paterl, coauthor of a 2010 report on the issue by the Brennan Center for Justice, the system doesn't really work when the courts, instead of administering justice, are debt-collection agencies. While there are no comprehensive data on how many states jail citizens for court-related debt, several organizations, including the Brennan Center, have raised alarms over what they say is the widespread practice of locking up offenders in violation of federal law, citing Supreme Court rulings that someone can only be incarcerated for "willfully" refusing to pay.[14]

Take the example of the registered nurse from Orange County, California. She was a single mother trying to make ends meet and raise her family. She was also dealing with various personal medical issues. While driving one day, her small child in a car seat in the back decided to unbuckle his car seat restraint to wave to the nice police officer driving behind his mother. For that friendly childish gesture, the officer pulled his mother over. When the officer was finished, Mom walked away with a $300 ticket for multiple driving offenses. She then missed her court appearance because of a surgery. The

$300 ticket quickly climbed to $3,000 because of interest, penalties, and a bench warrant for her arrest. Not knowing of the bench warrant, she continued to drive and live life. One day, a disturbance called the police to her apartment complex, and they asked for identification from everyone present. The nurse soon found herself in the back of a police car, not because of any crime she committed, but for the outstanding bench warrant for her traffic ticket. She spent three days in jail, missed work, and was brought before a judge. In the end, a judge cut her a break on the fines and gave her a sentence of time served, six months probation, and court costs. In addition to her penalty, her young children were without their mother for three nights, and she faced discipline at work for missing time off.[15]

Certain counties in Florida, Ohio, Georgia, and elsewhere also routinely imprison people who fail to keep up with court debt, according to the American Civil Liberties Union and the Brennan Center.[16] In practice, advocates said, courts often fail to inquire about a defendant's ability to pay until after they're incarcerated. Even states that do not regularly jail debtors may use the threat of jail to go after fees and fines, with consequences that can play out for years.

Ethan Bronner, a reporter for the *New York Times*, profiled thirty-one-year-old Gina Ray, who was fined $179 for a speeding ticket. Ray said that she did not show up in court because the ticket had the wrong date on it, and as a result of her failure to appear, her license was revoked, unbeknownst to her. At least until she found herself being pulled over by police for a moving violation. She was cited for operating without a license and was in much worse position.

Suddenly, her fees had increased nearly tenfold. She owed more than $1,500, and because she was unable to pay, she was handed over to a private probation company, jailed, and charged an additional fee for each day behind bars.[17]

BIG BUSINESS

The American prison system is massive. So massive, in fact, that its estimated turnover of $74 billion eclipses the GDP of 133 nations.[18] There are more prisoners than farmers in the US, with many prisons now in rural areas where farms once were.[19] Many American towns, once dependent on farming, mining, and manufacturing, are now wholly dependent on a prison. Another unsettling fact is that it is the American taxpayer who get billed, and we are all helping to pad the pockets of publicly traded corporations like Corrections Corporation of America (CCA) and GEO Group, which provides correctional and community reentry services. Combined, both of these companies generated over $2.53 billion in revenue in 2012 and represent more than half of the private prison business.[20]

So what exactly makes the business of incarcerating Americans so lucrative? The average cost of incarcerating an American prisoner varies from state to state. Some states, like Indiana, have managed to keep prices low at around $14,000 per inmate, while states like New York pay around $60,000 apiece to keep their citizens behind bars. According to a 2012 Vera Institute of Justice study, the number of those incarcerated has increased by over 700 percent over the last four decades, with the cost to the taxpayer of exceeding $39 billion.[21]

Without question, that cost burden is staggering, and it begs the logical question; what is all that taxpayer money being spent on?

The breakdown appears standard enough, with the Vera Institute contending that many corrections-related costs, such as employee benefits and taxes, pension contributions, retiree health care contributions, legal judgments, and claims, are deemed central administrative costs. Moreover, many states fund inmate services—such as hospital care in eight states, and education and training in 12 states—outside of their corrections departments. It's a nice accounting trick, but this amounts to a $5.5 billion gap between the reported corrections budgets of the forty states examined by the study—$33.5 billion—and the actual cost to the taxpayer of $39 billion.[22]

What this points to is the continued privatization of the prison industry. Competition in any work environment is, in theory, a good thing that should lead to lower costs across the board. The debate rages on regarding who can do a better job: the bureaucracy or private companies? Does it matter, or is it just about cost cutting? An interesting question, because privatization would save taxpayers a boatload of money in the renovation and building of new facilities, not to mention all the prison personnel to whom citizens would have to pay salaries and pensions in perpetuity.

Today, privatized prisons make up over 10 percent of the corrections market. Private prisons like CCA not only provide states and the federal government with lower "per-diem" costs, but they also provide a means for them to balance their budgets by buying off and refurbishing state-owned prisons. CCA operates the fifth-largest prison system, public or private, in the system in the US. Under its control are fifty-one owned-and-operated facilities in sixteen states and contracted management of eighteen more state-owned facilities in seven states. This network allows CCA to maintain a 44 percent stake in the $7.4 billion private corrections market for a market cap of $3.53 billion. All of this equates to a massively profitable operation for CCA, which recorded $1.64 billion in revenue, $883.1 million of which came from state governments in 2012.[23]

For Georgia teenager Kevin Thompson, a traffic ticket in 2015 ended up costing him not only his driver's license, but also his freedom. In his account of the experience, Thompson said he was ordered to pay $810 in fines, a sum he could not provide. As a consequence, his case was handed off to a for-profit probation company called Judicial Correction Services (JCS), which told Thompson he had thirty days to pay the fine, after which a JCS officer's recommendation to incarcerate him resulted in a five-day stint in jail for failure to pay his fine.[24]

Similar cases are coming to light all around the country as municipal courts increasingly outsource probation to for-profit companies.

The pitch is simple: A private company like JCS will help collect fines and fees owed to municipalities and courts that they might otherwise never see. These for-profit firms, called probation services companies, don't charge cities anything but instead put citizens who can't afford to pay fines, such as traffic tickets, on payment plans that slam them with exorbitant fees and then illegally threaten people with jail time if they fail to make payments.[25]

Thirteen states rely on for-profit probation companies such as JCS. More than 1,000 courts use private companies and sentence hundreds of thousands of Americans to probation each year, according to a report published last year by the Human Rights Watch, which called the trend an "offender-funded" model of privatized probation. In Georgia alone, thirty probation companies are working in more than 600 courts throughout the state, allowing them to collect almost $100 million in fines, court costs, restitution for those courts, and collections in 2012, the report noted.[26]

Inmates of debtors' prisons in the early American colonies, just like the ones across the ocean in England at the time, were forced to pay the cost of their incarceration and repay their debts, even though they were given no viable means or opportunity to pay off the debt. Entire communities sprang up inside the early debtors' prisons, which were run by private, for-profit institutions. Just as prison keepers used to charge inmates for food and board, and bailiffs charged for clothing, and attorneys charged legal fees, today we see companies like JCS, and others, collecting tens of millions of dollars in fines, court costs, and restitution from offenders for the courts.

Because for-profit probation companies tack on their own fees to the original municipal fines, this adds to the hurdles that people must jump over to try to erase the debt. Some people are forced to forgo groceries or default on other bills in order to save enough money to make the payments.[27]

In the ACLU's view, the relationship between municipalities and for-profit probation companies creates a financial incentive to generate profits at the expense of probationers' rights. In some cases, it may be the municipalities themselves that are seeking to drive up revenue collection from residents. The Department of Justice issued a scathing report about Ferguson, Missouri, which was the focus of protests and civil unrest last year over the fatal shooting of teenager Michael Brown by a police officer. The DOJ uncovered a pattern of emphasizing revenue collection by its police officers and municipal court. It's not only the failure to pay traffic tickets that is landing Americans in jails. Across the country, there are at any moment 730,000 people who are locked up in a local jail because they are unable to post bail.[28]

While a judge makes decisions about incarceration, it should be noted that the introduction of a for-profit company into the system can lead to incomplete and incorrect information from probation officers who aren't trained about constitutional rights.

The Human Rights Watch report noted that for-profit probation companies, while unable to send people to jail, routinely threatened to have them jailed for failing to make payments or for falling into arrears. The companies end up with a great deal of coercive power.[29]

If people who can't pay are incarcerated, it ends up costing the state more because it costs more to put them in prison than what they originally owed. Moreover, jail time can also accelerate a downward spiral for the debtors, because additional court costs are piled on top of their previous debts. That makes repayment even harder, and the cycle continues.

Some cities that have revived the use of debtors' prisons include Philadelphia, where courts in 2011 sought to collect on court-related debt from 320,000 people, involving obligations they owed dating back to the 1970s. Some judges, however, have had enough. An Alabama circuit court judge last year rebuked a municipal court and private probation company for incarcerating people over their criminal justice debt, calling the arrangement a judicially sanctioned extortion racket.[30]

However, such critiques are insufficient to lock the gates on debtors' prisons once and for all.

WORKING OFF DEBT

In Victorian debtors' prisons, inmates were given a chance to earn money for their creditors. As mentioned previously, prisoners from the master's side could also hire prisoners from the commoner side to act as their servants—how commoner prisoners would make money. Today, in the Albemarle-Charlottesville Regional Jail, inmates are being given a similar opportunity by being allowed to perform community service to work off the debt that they have racked up in fines and fees on their way through the court system. The community service option is open to those whose court debt is not tied to crimes that require jail time.

Under the debt-relief program, developed by the City of Charlottesville and two surrounding counties, the inmates' debt gets reduced by $7.25 per work hour, the state's minimum wage. Tasks include clearing trash and maintaining parks for various government agencies. The judges, prosecutors, court clerks, and jail administrators who developed the program say it helps to keep people from being thrown into a spiral of debt with little or no way of paying off their fines and fees, particularly as interest on the debt mounts. Charlottesville General District Judge Robert Downer Jr. acknowledged that it doesn't take long for court fines and fees to accumulate, and if people create a mountain that's too high to climb, then they give up hope. This program was established to allow people to meet their obligations and holds them accountable but gives them a way forward.[31]

New Mexico, Georgia, and Washington have similar programs aimed at helping people dig out from under court-ordered debt. Michigan allows people to reduce their debt by meeting education requirements, such as earning a GED diploma.

It makes one wonder why all states don't have debt reduction programs. It seems a win-win situation, with inmates lowering their debt and town halls getting a fresh coat of paint. The short answer, once again, is that courts in most states depend on the money they collect from fines and fees to keep the correction system machine running. With budgets being as tight as they are these days, it is political suicide to choke off a steady revenue source. In 2016, Oklahoma raised court fees to help cover costs.

Lauren-Brooke Eisen with the Brennan Center for Justice, which researches criminal justice issues, said the number of fees assessed nationally to fund a growing criminal justice system has been increasing. Some of these fees actually fund worthy causes, but defendants are paying for all these services and sometimes paying to keep lights in courthouses on, so it is not the most efficient or just use of resources. When people can't pay in Virginia, for instance, it's state policy to suspend the debtors' driver's licenses. Currently, more than 940,000 Virginians have lost their licenses to debt, a practice that, as we know, only compounds the problem, because often not being able to drive results in job loss and no way to pay the original debt. Many people, continue to drive after their license has been suspended and, if they are caught multiple times, end up in jail.[32]

One lawmaker in Florida is interested in creating community service opportunities for offenders but additionally would like to end the practice of suspending driver's licenses when people can't pay court debt. And herein lies the dilemma, with the question of how to pay for such a program. Court Clerks in Florida have warned legislators that if they approve a community service debt-relief program, they may have to plug a multimillion-dollar gap in court funding. They estimate that if just 15 percent of inmates in the state opt to perform community service rather than pay fines and fees, the courts will lose $25 million a year.[33]

Taking a different approach, there are those who advocate for completely doing away with fees and fines because so many people cannot pay them. They argue that financial penalties don't serve their intended purpose.

In Tennessee, for example, it is estimated that the collection rate was 72 percent in civil courts and 30 percent in criminal courts. State legislators here are pushing for the creation of a state council to review fees. Since 2005, the state has passed forty-six bills that increased or added new fees, creating a patchwork of fees at different levels of the courts that is difficult to untangle.[34]

Inmates performing community service have another added benefit that is even more important, and that is simply giving people who are unemployed a chance to make a living when they are released. The training and connections they make through their service are invaluable to many inmates. Whether helping out the parks department by clearing trails and painting over graffiti; or spending the day with the local branch of the state Department of Transportation, clearing roads of trash and debris; or even working as a flagger, controlling traffic while crews are working, inmates are given a skill they did not have before they were jailed. Some of these jobs require taking a class to become certified, giving them a new avenue for employment upon their release. That's important, for the offender and the community.

The Charlottesville jail superintendent has said that their program saves both the local government and the state money. Since 2012, he calculates, the 61,000 working hours that inmates have put in at $7.25 an hour have saved the governments more than $900,000 by not having to hire temporary employees to do the same work at $15 an hour.[35]

If that's not a win-win, nothing is. These are the kinds of programs that should be adopted in every county across the country to end the use of incarceration to collect debt.

8

TILL DEBT DUE US PART

In America, there are more than 800,000 divorces each year.[1] Many of them involve families with children, and this inevitably leads to a multitude of court orders regarding child support, medical coverage, and alimony, all of which are legitimate provisions deserving of spouses and the children in their care. The problems begin when the orders exceed a person's ability to pay, which is not uncommon. Then, when the payments are not made, courts have numerous means at their disposable to ensure that this money be collected, including garnishing up to 65 percent of a person's gross income, seizing bank deposits and tax refunds, suspending drivers and professional licenses, and, finally, imprisonment for contempt.[2]

Sometimes, divorce can be a big factor in the filing of personal bankruptcy, even if it's just due to the fact that two people will no longer be contributing to pay debts they had accrued together. Bankruptcy becomes a way to protect your family as well as yourself, and to allow for a fresh start. That said, crimes involving bankruptcy are on the rise in America, and the threat of jail omnipresent. A person filing for bankruptcy is providing information to the court under penalty of perjury, and this offense is punishable for up to five years in prison.

HOW TO DEAL WITH MARITAL DEBT BEFORE IT BECOMES A PROBLEM

Marital debt, just like marital assets, is invariably split in some way during divorce. Something not as well understood, though, is the fact that a contract you have with a debtor doesn't change, irrespective of who was ordered to pay which debt.

In other words, if your name is on a car loan or home mortgage, you will continue to be held responsible postdivorce for those debts.

The only agreement a creditor has to abide by is the one you signed with him. It doesn't matter if your final decree of divorce states that your ex is to pay the car loan. That does not release you from your obligation for the loan. It is for this reason that couples should pay off as many debts as possible before filing for a divorce. If your ex is ordered to pay debts X, Y, and Z, and fails to do so, a creditor will come after you if your name is also on the loan agreement.[3] That is the most important thing you need to know when it comes to dividing debt during the divorce process. There may be some debts that you are not aware of, however. For instance, if you live in a community property state, you can be held responsible for debt incurred by your spouse even if you were unaware of the debt and did not sign an agreement with a creditor. In other words, in a community property state, marital debt is considered joint debt, or debt for which you are both responsible. A creditor can come after you for payment of a debt you did not create. Full financial disclosure is important during settlement negotiations to help protect yourself if you live in these states. You should make a detailed list of all account numbers, amounts owed, and who is responsible for each of the debts. Ordering a copy of your credit report can help you get started.[4]

These are things you can control. But what if your ex doesn't pay, how can you protect yourself from that situation?

Let's say, for example, the marital debt will be split equally between you and your ex. You are to pay half, and your ex is to pay the other half. What can you do if you pay your share, but your ex does not pay the other half? The truth is that you can't do anything unless you have an indemnity clause added to your divorce settlement agreement during negotiations. To protect your credit rating, you have to pay both halves. If worded properly, an indemnity clause will allow you to take your ex back to court for any money you had to pay as a result of the loan going into default. Consult with your lawyer about this before signing the final papers.[5] The old adage by Benjamin Franklin, "An ounce of prevention is worth a pound of cure," in this instance will save you a lot of money and stress.

When it comes to secured loans, it is always safe to refinance them before filing. It is common for a divorce attorney to suggest that you have your name removed from the title of a marital home or automobile. However, do this if there is an outstanding loan and your name is on the loan agreement.

You should insist that any property that is still under a finance agreement be refinanced in your spouse's name alone. For example, if your ex is going to keep the car and the loan is in both names, your name needs to be removed from the loan, and this can only be done if he or she refinances the loan. Furthermore, make sure that there is language in your final decree of divorce that states the property is to be refinanced along with the time period in which he or she is to complete the refinance. It is wise to include language in your divorce decree that states the consequences to your ex if he or she does not follow through with refinancing the property. For example, if your ex remained in the family home and is supposed to refinance the home into his or her name within six months of the divorce and doesn't do so, the home will be put on the market and sold. Knowing that he or she may lose property can often motivate an ex to do the right thing.[6]

When it comes right down to it, the final decree of divorce is nothing more than a promise on a piece of paper. Just because a judge signs it and your ex is ordered to follow it does not mean he or she will. What you have to do is think of all the possibilities and how to protect yourself in any situation that may arise once you are divorced. To do so, you must start by paying off as much debt as possible before filing for divorce; make sure you are aware of all debt in both names. And add an indemnity clause to your divorce settlement agreement if needed to make sure debt your ex is ordered to pay is refinanced.[7]

DIVORCE AND DEBT

Unfortunately, divorce and bankruptcy seem to go hand in hand for some people. The two often occur in tandem, and understanding that can lessen the impact and help you decide whether you should file for bankruptcy before or after your divorce.

It's no secret that divorce is an overwhelming, stressful event in most people's lives. Besides lawyer and court costs, you and your spouse will probably be expected to cover the expenses of two households rather than just one. And if one spouse must now find a new job, childcare costs may come into play.

From 1980 to 2008, statistics on bankruptcy filing show that more than 90 percent of filers experienced job loss or medical hardship during their divorce. This suggests that such financial stressors may frequently lead Americans to file for bankruptcy. Depending on the laws of your state (community property or equitable distribution), you may find yourself owning less property and more debt than you did before your marriage.[8]

Complicating these financial concerns further, many divorces today include orders for alimony or child support. For people struggling to get by on just one income, their paycheck just won't stretch far enough to meet these obligations and still be able to pay the other bills. Hence, bankruptcy often enters into many divorce proceedings. So if your spouse starts bankruptcy proceedings before the judge finalizes your divorce, you might want to think about jointly filing for bankruptcy, especially if the majority of your debt obligations are in both your names. As mentioned, because a creditor is not considered a party to a divorce agreement, you will still be responsible for the joint debts, even if your husband is the only one declaring bankruptcy. If you jointly file for bankruptcy before your divorce, you'll be able to avoid many of the headaches involved in negotiating the division of assets and debts, because most of this will have been settled by the bankruptcy proceedings.[9]

It's important to note that a joint bankruptcy filing is typically not available to divorced couples, even if much of their debts are held jointly. For this reason, if you are contemplating bankruptcy and haven't yet filed for a divorce, you should consider consulting with a bankruptcy lawyer before dissolving your marriage. Bankruptcy can actually help struggling divorcees, and it is typically done in one of two ways. Chapter 13 bankruptcy is a type of personal bankruptcy that allows petitioners a period of three to five years to get current on their past-due debts by making regular payments in a structured repayment plan. It tends to work best for people who have a dependable income source and/or significant nonexempt assets or property they want to keep. On the other hand, Chapter 7 bankruptcy is a type of personal bankruptcy that offers petitioners a complete discharge of many unsecured debts (debts not attached to any property). Keep in mind, though, that the ways in which the debts are designated by the divorce court may not hold up in a bankruptcy court. For example, if a spouse is assigned a joint debt in the divorce and then files for Chapter 7 bankruptcy, the creditors can still come after the other spouse for repayment. Because of the possibility of one spouse being held responsible for debts that were assigned to the other spouse during divorce, it's important to contact your ex-spouse if you're considering a bankruptcy filing.[10]

But bankruptcy can't eliminate all debts. If you saw your income decrease after the terms of your divorce were settled, you may be worried about keeping up with support payments as well as your mortgage/rent and regular bills. But the place to modify the terms of your divorce is probably in the divorce court, not the bankruptcy court. The following debts are not dischargeable in bankruptcy, meaning that filing for bankruptcy will not likely relieve you of your responsibility to pay: child support, alimony/spousal maintenance, student loans, most tax debt, and some criminal fines and penalties. If you need help in resolving any of these debt scenarios, you need not despair, because bankruptcy may offer you relief by possibly excusing you from other debts, leaving you with enough money to cover your support or maintenance payments. It may be just a matter of seeking help by speaking with a bankruptcy lawyer in your area.[11]

DEADBEAT DEBTORS

According to a *Wall Street Journal* article by Emeritus Professor Gordon E. Finley, PhD, a professor of psychology at Florida International University in Miami, the only US citizens who can be imprisoned for debt are fathers in arrears for child support. The parent-to-prison pathway generally goes something like this: fall behind in child support, and the state takes away all professional and drivers' licenses. This makes it impossible for fathers to generate income, and so the arrears increase, the father goes to debtors' prison, and with a prison record it becomes difficult to near impossible to ever get a job in the aboveground economy. The future prospects of the children of imprisoned fathers are uniformly bleak, especially when compounded with the well-established findings that children from single-mother families have the worst developmental outcomes of all family forms.[12]

The phrase "deadbeat dad" is a familiar one, and even though this pejorative term of deadbeat is sometimes even used in the actual legislation of some states, it is often misused and misunderstood. The first thing is that unpaid child support can also be attributed to women. When a parent is ordered by the court to pay regular child support, yet fails to do so over and over again, he or she is commonly referred to as a "deadbeat parent." However, not all parents who've fallen behind on child support payments are willfully refusing to support their children financially, as some parents fall behind on child support due to job loss or other serious unforeseen circumstances. So the term *deadbeat* is usually reserved for those who have the means to pay but choose not to. Parents who want to support their children, but are legitimately unable to pay, may be eligible for child support modification.[13]

When parents find themselves in arrears simply because they do not have the money, their child support payments can be legally adjusted accordingly to reflect their current earnings.

The parent sometimes owes so much child support that the money will simply never be paid in full. To address this concern, some states have begun to offer child support amnesty programs where the accumulated fines associates with unpaid child support can be reduced while the parent begins to make back payments.

The Spruce, a home website offering tips and home advice, reported that statistically fewer than 50 percent of the children who are owed child support money regularly receive full payments. That's why failure to pay child support is a federal offense in the eyes of the US government. In fact, a noncustodial parent who fails to pay child support in full and on time faces several penalties. In an effort to minimize the impact of unpaid child support, states impose a number of penalties against parents who fall behind on child support payments, including having your driver's license suspended. States now ask if you pay child support when you get or renew your driver's license. In addition, local child support agencies regularly communicate with the Division of Motor Vehicles when a parent falls behind on child support payments, allowing the state to quickly enforce this first-step penalty for failure to pay child support.[14]

A parent who is delinquent on his or her child support payments may have wages garnished. This means that the state will contact the employer directly and have them take payments right out of that person's paycheck. This particular penalty is generally viewed as an embarrassment and could even influence the parent's status at work. States regularly charge additional fines and penalties for unpaid child support, and this is why so many parents who fall behind on regular payments wind up owing tens of thousands of dollars. Deadbeat parents will likely find that they are unable to obtain a passport. The state can prevent them from obtaining or renewing their passports in order to limit their ability to travel for work or leisure. Dismissal from military service is also a possibility. Single parents in the military who fail to pay child support may be dismissed from military service as a consequence for nonpayment. And in some cases, imprisonment is a real possibility for failing to pay child support, even if it is a last resort. The length of time spent in jail varies by jurisdiction. Unfortunately, while severe, this penalty also means that the parent cannot work during this time, which only compounds the family's hardship. Therefore, parents who go to jail for nonpayment rarely emerge from jail better equipped to address the issue and start making regular child support payments.[15]

Not everything is black and white when you look at each child support case individually. Because there are shades of gray, requiring discretionary consideration, there are additional penalties that can be levied for a parent who fails to pay child support.

The federal government takes strong issue with parents who attempt to work the system and avoid child support payments. In cases where a noncustodial parent who is charged with child support nonpayment moves to a different state to avoid making child support payments, he or she may be convicted of a federal offense under the Deadbeat Parents Punishment Act, a bill signed into law by President Bill Clinton in 1998. The Act entails felony punishment for a parent who relocates to another state, or country, with the intention of evading child support payments. Prior to 1998, the law deemed it a misdemeanor to cross state lines to avoid payments. In order to secure a conviction under the Deadbeat Parents Punishment Act, the federal government must prove that the parent had the ability to pay child support, that that parent willfully failed to pay, that the child support had not been paid for at least a year, and that the parent owed more than $5,000 in child support.[16] Parents who owe $10,000 or more, or who fail to pay for two years, could face up to two years in prison. Parents could also face fines and would be responsible for making restitution for unpaid child support. Conversely, for those times when a parent legitimately cannot make child support payments due to a sudden job loss or other legitimate financial hardship, there is amnesty. However, parents should never fail to make child support payments altogether without communicating with the other parent and the state about the issue. Parents who struggle with child support payments should try to work something out with the local child support agency or seek a formal child support modification through the courts. It is recommended that, to the best of their ability, they should continue to provide support in other ways. For example, by providing clothing, food, medical care, and child care. In addition, they should remember that making partial child support payments is better than no payment at all.[17]

THE EFFECTIVENESS OF JAILING DEADBEAT PARENTS

According to Jonathan Walters, senior editor of Governing.com, a media platform covering politics, policy, and management for state and local government leaders, throwing someone in jail for not paying their bills has never proved to be very effective at getting anyone to pay what they owe. After all, if you're in jail, you certainly aren't making any money. Yet for those who fail to come up with child support, holding them in contempt and tossing them into jail is still the standard avenue of recourse.[18]

The good news is that some in the human services field are starting to pursue a more enlightened course when it comes to dealing with deadbeat parents. Vicki Turetsky, who was commissioner at the federal Office of Child Support Enforcement (OCSE), began a push for more programs that help noncustodial parents find jobs, hang on to them, and ultimately meet their child support obligations. Back in 2012, the OCSE launched demonstration projects in eight states that Turetsky hoped would encourage parents' ability and willingness to pay. She made a case for such programs during a forum hosted by the American Public Human Services Association. The idea behind these demonstration projects was "to go from punishing nonpaying, noncustodial parents to working and back into the family fold, at least financially, through a more cooperative and holistic approach," which includes much closer coordination between child support enforcement offices and children and family services agencies.[19]

There were some technical fixes that the OCSE wanted to see made to the process, as well. One of those changes involved the fees that governments skim off of child support payments to pay administrative costs. Turetsky's office wanted to have 100 percent of child support payments go to the families. As a powerful disincentive to getting men to pay up, the government skimming leads them to take jobs where they are paid in cash so as to stay under the state's income-reporting radar. Getting income right is important, and using an individual's real income as opposed to computed income would go a long way to encourage compliance. Overall, the focus of these projects remains on employing a softer approach, reducing contempt hearings, and increasing positive strategies for engaging fathers in the hope that such engagement may even move beyond just finances. Essentially, child support shouldn't strictly be a law enforcement issue, but rather should follow other trends in children and family services and swing around to a softer, more engagement- and employment-oriented approach.[20]

While this approach might seem groundbreaking or unique, many jurisdictions have been turning away from penalties and sanctions in these cases and looking toward alternative means to arrive at a more effective resolution to this problem.

As an example, in Texas, where child support enforcement is under the aegis of the attorney general, the AG's office has launched a program called Noncustodial Parent Choices (NPC), which serves noncustodial parents who are behind in support payments by removing barriers to employment and helping fathers become economically self-sufficient. The program was deemed "highly successful," according to a US OCSE report, bringing in nearly $30 million in its first four years of operation. And New York's Office of Temporary and Disability Assistance has piloted NPC-like employment programs in four cities and found that participants earned significantly more than the control group, resulting in equally significant increases in child support payments. And in Wake County, North Carolina, those ordered by the court into a work program have increased their child support payments over time, while those ordered straight to jail didn't, according to the OCSE report.[21]

The examples seem to illustrate that strong-arming and detaining deadbeat parents does not result in more money being provided to the children of these families.

In an April 2015 edition of the *New York Times* opinion page, a writer expressed a similar and very poignant view on this matter, namely, that for a long time, advocates for the poor have complained that the punitive enforcement measures used by state child support systems were counterproductive in providing continuing support for many children. The primary focus on punishing deadbeat parents has obscured the unintended consequences for low-income families. Now it seems that the tragic killing of Walter L. Scott in South Carolina has shed light on a system desperately in need of a policy overhaul.[22]

The Walter Scott case involved the tragic shooting death of an unarmed black man on April 4, 2015, by North Charleston police officer Michael Slager following a daytime traffic stop for a nonfunctioning brake light. The race difference led many to believe that the shooting was racially motivated, generating a widespread controversy. Slager was charged with murder after a video surfaced that showed him shooting Scott from behind while Scott was fleeing, and that contradicted his police report. A South Carolina Grand Jury indicted Slager on a charge of murder, and the following year, a five-week trial ended in a mistrial due to a hung jury. In May 2016, Slager was indicted on federal charges including violation of Scott's civil rights and obstruction of justice. In a plea agreement the following year, Slager pleaded guilty to federal charges of civil rights violations. In return for his guilty plea, the murder charges from the state were dropped.

Incarcerating those who owe child support, the *New York Times* Op letter went on to say, is almost never a rational response for failure to pay. There are numerous enforcement tools available to states to compel payments when noncustodial parents have the ability to pay but won't. If they can't pay, jail is ineffective for generating child support and serves as a mechanism to punish parents for being poor. Incarceration has a devastating effect on the long-term employability of parents saddled with a criminal conviction. Studies have shown that a criminal record has a significant impact on a parent's ability to get and maintain meaningful employment and diminishes earning capacity for the rest of his or her life. For parents who are already having difficulty keeping up with child payments, this is a recipe for further instability. The child support system is intended to provide needed financial and emotional support for children, not to punish parents. Policies that work at cross-purposes with this important goal need a second look.[23]

The woman who expressed these thoughts was a professor at the City University of New York School of Law and the author of numerous articles on the policy implications of low-income incarcerated parents with child support debt. The emotional and financial toll is high for families. Incarcerated parents are often separated from their children by long distances and for long periods of time, and the emotional and financial toll is high for families, especially for children. Researchers at Child Trends—a nonprofit research center that studies children with the aim of improving their outcomes by collecting research, data, and analysis—acknowledges several longitudinal studies of the long-term impact of parental incarceration on children. Their data show an alarming collection of "adverse childhood experiences (ACEs)" affecting children with incarcerated parents. The list of such ACEs includes increased risk for trauma, or toxic stress, particularly when it is cumulative.

For example, children with an incarcerated parent are much more likely to experience divorce and witness substance abuse and violence in their homes or neighborhoods.

Incarcerating noncustodial parents for failure to pay child support is not an effective enforcement strategy for parents earning little or no income, according to Melissa Young, director of National Initiatives on Poverty and Economic Opportunity for Heartland Alliance for Human Needs and Human Rights. A better strategy is connecting these parents to employment. For noncustodial parents with child support debt, there are work-oriented programs that couple job training with innovative strategies, helping parents break the cycle of unemployment, debt, and imprisonment. These strategies include helping parents reinstate driver's licenses so they can get to work, modifying child support orders to reflect actual ability to pay, and brokering debt compromises that reduce state-owed child support debt. For millions of noncustodial parents, it's employment, not incarceration, that will help them support their families while meeting their own needs.[24]

BAD JUDGMENT

When collection agents use the threat of jail when trying to collect from debtors who owe them, this often sends the debtor running to a bankruptcy attorney for protection. Such action usually turns out to be just the resolution the debtor was seeking, but there are a growing number of incidents across the United States of debtors being thrown in jail related to nonpayment of a debt.

A 2014 *Boston Globe* article by Walter V. Robinson revealed a particularly disturbing ruling by a judge in Boston who put a man in jail because he wouldn't repay a $500 debt he was ordered to repay. As an attorney, I find the case fascinating, and as a person, I find it appalling.

Iheanyi D. Okoroafor, a 73-year-old retiree, was taken away in handcuffs because he had not paid a debt of $508.27. As he was being escorted out of the courtroom, he turned to Belchertown District Court Judge Robert S. Murphy Jr. and told him that his wife was in the hospital and that he needed to go to her. The judge, who found Okoroafor in contempt and sentenced him to thirty days in jail for defying a small-claims order to pay a debt to a local heating contractor, Boisjolie, did not respond to the defendant. Judge Murphy's decision that Okoroafor had the money to settle the debt was based on the fact that Okoroafor received a $2,000 monthly state pension. Under state law, however, state pensions cannot be considered by the court as income when calculating whether a defendant has the resources to pay off such a debt. Compounding this apparent error, the judge made his decision without asking whether Okoroafor had a bank account and, if so, whether it held any funds. At the time, besides having a sick wife, the defendant had fallen behind on his utility bills, and three months previously he said he began weekly visits to an Amherst food bank because he did not have sufficient income to buy enough food. He also told the judge that he tithed, donating $200 from his pension to his church each month, a disclosure that the judge seemed to take as evidence that Okoroafor could pay the debt.[25]

The State Retirement Board and other experts in debt collection agreed that the Massachusetts statute that exempts state pension income from debtor judgments is clear. One law professor said that even if the income were not exempt, it was particularly egregious that the judge sent Okoroafor to jail, given his age, family circumstances, and size of the debt. The spokeswoman for the courthouse issued a statement afterward, stating that the applicability of a statute is a legal question decided by judges in the context of a particular case, and that judges apply the law to the facts they deem credible in rendering decisions.[26]

Court officials said they have no way to track how often this happens, but contempt citations and jail sentences are considered rare in debt collection cases and rarer still if the debtor is elderly or infirm.

While Okoroafor, to some, is not a sympathetic figure, his attitude and actions regarding his debt are well documented. Okoroafor, who emigrated from Nigeria in 1978, has a doctorate in education from the University of Massachusetts. Before he retired in 2007, he was a supervisor in the state Department of Mental Health. Over the course of the eighteen months prior to the decision, Okoroafor had written several angry letters denouncing the contractor, South Hadley's Board of Health, and its Police Department, asserting there was a conspiracy against him. Okoroafor insisted all along that he should not have to pay Boisjolie because the contractor did not do the work but billed him anyway. He even sent a complaint to a prior judge in the case, threatening to report him to the Judicial Conduct Commission.[27]

The case left the judge in an awkward position. In the District Courts, where staff has been cut by 16 percent since 2006, judges, while handling large criminal caseloads, must do their own legal research. Even against that backdrop, it has been asserted that Murphy and his colleagues are supposed to know the intricacies of debt collection law, including which income is exempt from judgment. Small-claims cases like Okoroafor's seldom require the intervention of judges, with court clerks usually adjudicating the disputes.[28]

Back in 2013, Boisjolie won a default judgment because Okoroafor did not show up for a hearing. Okoroafor's subsequent hand-crafted motions to set aside the judgment and hold a hearing were denied. When the case returned to court, Judge Murphy apparently misunderstood another judge's notes in the case file, thinking the previous judge had ordered, not simply advised, Okoroafor to hire a lawyer if he refused to pay up. In court, Murphy asked Okoroafor if he had found a lawyer. The defendant said he had tried but could not afford one. The dilemma here is that no judge can order a defendant, especially a small-claims defendant, to hire an attorney, particularly because the cost of doing so would easily exceed the amount of the debt. On the narrow merits of the case, Okoroafor and the two judges whose patience he tested at the successive hearings often seemed to be talking past one another. They kept asking why he had flouted several court orders over a year's time to pay the debt. He, in turn, kept insisting that he did not owe the debt because the contractor never did the work in question and had proof of that if they would only grant him a hearing on the merits. When Okoro-afor was asked in court a final time why he could not pay the debtor, the defendant repeated that the contractor did not do the job.[29]

The judge found Okoroafor in contempt and sentenced him to thirty days in jail for defying a small-claims order to pay his debt to the local heating contractor. Okoroafor was freed at about 2 a.m. the next day after his daughter, Amara Okoroafor, drove from Boston to the Hampshire County Jail in Northampton and paid the debt.

But Judge Murphy was insistent that the court's decision to order him to pay was the right one, and that was final. Okoroafor had no choice but to pay up or wind up in contempt for willfully refusing to pay a debt that he was deemed to have the ability to pay.

It is cases like these that make people upset, and it is understandable. It makes me upset to hear them. The power to talk about such injustices is the first step, but something more needs to be done about them. Debt should not cause additional hardship and heartache.

The Okoroafor case raises larger issues for the court, expressing concern that judges may not be knowledgeable enough to know when certain income, like state pensions, is exempt from judgments, and that other debtors may have been ordered to pay debts from income that is legally walled off from court judgments. The court system is set up to be adversarial, where lawyers ordinarily oppose one another, but when one party is unrepresented, it's especially important that the court know and apply the law correctly.[30]

For Okoroafor, the court experience has been a traumatic exclamation point on an almost two-year-long saga. His wife, Evelyn, is coping with dementia, and he can no longer care for her at home. The elderly couple had to relocate, leaving Massachusetts to move in with their daughter, who lives in Maryland. It was the only way for them to get by.

9

JAILING
LOW-INCOME DEBTORS

THE STORY OF Danny Bearden is rewritten in courts across the country today on a daily and weekly basis. Also, as discussed in Chapter 2, the protections our Supreme Court established in *Bearden v. Georgia* are trampled upon by State Courts. Court costs have increased in both size and scope over the last thirty years across the nation. State and county governments are more aggressive in the collection efforts of court debt from people who have already served criminal sentences or have gotten caught violating motor vehicle offenses, regardless of their ability to pay. Courts primarily collect outstanding court debt from defendants by creating payment plans and issuing arrest warrants for people who do not appear to make payments. Our nation has seen an increase in these collections efforts because of finances or lack thereof.

The Social Security Administration set the median household income in America at $56,561 in 2015. The Census Bureau tells us the average family has approximately 3.14 people in it. Now let's take the average family at the average income level. The cost of living, child care expenses, and education force the average family to struggle to make ends meet when they only take home a little over $1,000 prior to income tax deductions. On the way to work one day, after dropping their child to daycare, they are running late and get pulled over for speeding while trying to make it on time. The officer writes the person a ticket for, say, $200. Now the person is going to be late for work because of the traffic stop, and his pay will be docked. Second, the family now has a decision to make: do they pay the ticket by mail for $200? Paying the ticket by mail means an admission to the charge and probably an increase in insurance premiums. If he wants to fight the ticket or ask a judge for leniency, he is going to have to take a day (or part of) out of work, causing his pay to be docked further. Now, paying the ticket may mean not paying another household bill, such as electricity or heat. So the family puts the ticket off for another day or another week, hoping for the chance of working overtime or the chance of a windfall. Putting off the ticket, missing a court date, and hoping the ticket goes away on its own. The court defaults the person and sends a license suspension notice for failure to pay the fine. Now his license to operate a motor vehicle is suspended. The dad in this family continues to drive because he needs to go to work to help support his family. This goes on for months, perhaps years, until he is stopped again or he gets into an accident. His license is suspended, and he is charged with driving on a suspended license. He is still making the same income and is now faced with a crime in many states. The only way to get his license back is to pay the old speeding ticket and now pay more fines and court costs. His license stays suspended, and he can't afford to pay the mounting fines, court costs, and possible probation costs imposed. When he can't pay the court debts and misses more court payment dates because he needs to go to work, a warrant is issued for his arrest. The police then pick him up on a Friday night for an outstanding warrant, and he is kept over the weekend in the local jail for a court appearance on Monday morning. Missing work, forced to pay some money to get out of jail, and mounting fees and interest. The original ticket now caused more missed time from work, and the fines have tripled, with a weekend in jail, a suspended license, increased insurance premiums, and possibly the jeopardy of losing his job. This cycle is the debilitating position many Americans face throughout our country.

Now imagine you live in poverty and you are faced with the above scenario. Daily, indigent people are jailed for failing to pay legal financial obligations they can never afford to pay. In many instances, people end up in jail or are threatened with incarceration with no attorney representation. These actions by the courts fly in the face of *Bearden v. Georgia,* the equal protection clause, and more recently a March 2016 United States Department of Justice letter penned by Karol Mason, an assistant attorney general; Vanita Gupta, principal deputy assistant attorney general of the Civil Rights Division; and Lisa Foster, the director of the Office for Access to Justice. The March 2016 letter reasserts it is unlawful for state court systems to arrest and incarcerate debtors for failure to pay court dates without first assessing the ability to pay. However, even with these protections in place, courts continue to lock up people for being poor, creating illegal sentences; further hardships for people who may already struggle with the effects of incarceration; and the waste of time and money on efforts to attempt to get payments from people who are unemployed, homeless, or simply have no means to pay their debt.

In *Fant v. City of Furgeson*, class-action members brought suit against the City, alleging the Ferguson jails were modern-day debtors' prisons that create a vicious cycle of continually jailing the poor for years. The Department of Justice issued a report on the Ferguson Police Department and how their priority was not safety oriented, but their priority was raising revenue. Incarcerating the poor for failure to pay fines is a national problem. Our country leads the world in incarceration rates but only has 5 percent of the world's population. While many people in our country have knowledge of the mass incarceration problem, few know of the return of debtors' prisons. Some may have only heard of them as described by Charles Dickens. While jails are not built strictly to house debtors anymore, debtors are still being incarcerated for not paying their financial obligations. Making matters worse, many of the collection efforts have been outsourced to private probation companies who also charge and assess fees. They use the threat of incarceration as a scare tactic to improve their collection efforts. Indigents are sent to jail despite the Supreme Court decisions stating they should not be incarcerated for their inability to pay. These actions hit the poor and minorities the hardest. Those who are lucky enough to pay their fines escape the system, leaving behind the poorest to rack up further late fees and interest. Therefore, the people who are least able to pay end up with more debt than those who can afford to pay their debt immediately. Many indigents pay more than just fines and interest; they pay dearly when they lose their jobs, get evicted from their homes, and end up with suspended licenses. And so the vicious circle of poverty continues.

The American Civil Liberties Union has been at the forefront of the debtors' prison issue for several years. In October 2010, the ACLU issued close to a 100-page report titled *In For A Penny: The Rise of America's New Debtors' Prisons*, which was a result of a yearlong investigation into the state of debtors' prisons in America. In that report, they highlight various noteworthy examples of people being incarcerated in five different states around the country. First, in Louisiana, the report cites the example of Sean Matthews, a construction worker who has no home, is living with friends and relatives, and was convicted of a possession of marijuana charge in 2007. For the conviction, the Court imposed a $300 fine, $148 in court costs, and a $50 assessment for the Law Enforcement Fund. Unable to pay the fines, Matthews was arrested two years later on a warrant. Weeks and months went by, Matthews continued to sit in jail, and no one could tell him when he would be brought to court. Finally, approximately five months later, he was brought before a judge, when his fines and fees were waived and he was finally released.[1] The report raises and, more important, illustrates the larger questionable issue and inefficiency seen throughout this country. For every day Matthews spent languishing in jail until someone figured out that he had to be brought to court, his detainment cost the City of New Orleans $22.39 per day. For the total time he spent in jail, it cost the City $3,201.77 in reimbursements to the prison, more than six times the $498 financial debt Matthews owed in the first place.[2] Not to mention the time and money spent by or paid to law enforcement, correctional officers, court clerks, and a judge that it took to bring Mr. Matthews before the Court in the first place. Sean Matthews was only one of many egregious examples in Louisiana brought to light in the ACLU report.

In Michigan, the 2010 ACLU report details the case of Kawana Young, a twenty-five-year-old single mother of two young sons. In 2005, Ms. Young received her first-ever traffic offense for not having her driver's license in her possession. In the following years, she received more traffic-related offenses from driving with loud music and having expired plates. Being in and out of employment over the course of a few years, Ms. Young couldn't afford to pay the fines. Five years after her first offense, Young was pulled over and taken into custody on three outstanding warrants for failure to pay. She had her children in the car at the time and had to make arrangements to have the children picked up and cared for. She spent the night in jail and was told by a judge the next day she had to pay $300 to secure her release or she would spend three days in jail on one of the warrants. The judge refused to place her on a payment plan when she explained that she wasn't trying to escape the debt but had no means to pay at the current time.[3] Therefore, she spent three days in jail and incurred a booking fee and a daily fee for her cost of incarceration. After the three days, she was ordered to pay additional $400 for her second of three warrants. In all, Ms. Young was sent to jail five times due to inability to pay fines. To make matters worse, she fell behind on her rent and paying bare necessities to care for her two sons. Not to mention the explanation that must have been needed to her two sons why their Mom was sent to jail. The report goes on further to detail other cases where people in Michigan were sent to jail for failing to pay legal obligations even though they were on disability, unemployed, and receiving other social service payments.

In Ohio, the ACLU report illustrates the case of Howard Webb as a prime example of abuse of judicial power. In 2006, Mr. Webb was taken into custody and charged with contempt of court for failing to make payments on fines and court costs from nine criminal and traffic offenses in a Municipal

Court. At the time of his arrest, Webb was a dishwasher making $7.00 per hour and was paying $118.23 for child support every two weeks. Previously, he was on disability, as well. His total financial legal obligation was $2,882.36 for fines and costs that had grown due to warrants and interest over the years.[4] In 2000, Webb spent 114 days in jail when Judge Goldie revoked his probation and would not give him credit for time served toward the fines by Ohio Statute that require a $50 per day credit off the fines for each day served in jail. In 2002, Webb served another thirty days for contempt, and in 2005 he received sixty more days for failure to pay. Through 2005, Mr. Webb served 204 days in jail, despite repeated attempts to make payment plans and be released so he could secure employment to pay the fines. If the judge had followed the law, Mr. Webb's jail time should have paid off $10,200 in fines and costs pursuant to the State Law that allows a $50 credit per day for every day served.[5] However, that didn't happen, and Judge Goldie sentenced Webb to another 270 days in 2006. Finally, the Court of Appeals heard Mr. Webb's case and dismissed it along with all financial obligations. But the real question is how does Howard Webb get that time back? Time missed from work and with his family. Not to mention the embarrassment the Court brought upon him to make him look like a person of ill repute. As for Judge Goldie, she was later publicly reprimanded for imposing jail upon people in disregard for State Law.[6]

The ACLU spotlighted a case from Georgia in their 2010 report, a state where statistics suggest a disproportionate number of African Americans are affected by debtors' prisons. While African Americans consist of 30 percent of Georgia's population, they are the majority in the State prison population.[7] Mr. Frank Hatley of Georgia spent a total of nineteen months in jail for nonpayment of child support for a child that wasn't even his.[8] In fact, he has no biological children. For eleven years, he thought he did have a child and made regular child support payments. In 2000, a DNA test concluded the child he thought was his was in fact not his own. When the DNA proved otherwise, the Court stopped all future payments but continued to make him obligated for the back support payments that had accrued when he thought the child was his. Hatley had small earnings and unemployment benefits at the time and used those to try to pay the arrears. While unemployed, he fell behind on payments and was jailed for six months in 2006. Then in 2008, Mr. Hately, on unemployment and living out of his car, fell behind on the past child support payments. Again, he was sent to jail. Finally, through the assistance of a human rights attorney, the Superior Court saw the injustice and relieved Hately of all his past child support obligations and ordered his release after he served more than a year in jail. In the end, the man regained his freedom and his debt was resolved, but the cost in terms of the valuable time he lost with his family and the public humiliation he suffered could never be recouped.

As seen since the days of the old English debtors' prisons, not only the debtors themselves are affected, but the families of the debtors sometimes take the brunt of the punishment. The ACLU report points out an example of how a parent of a minor, who also is a leading criminal justice advocate for children, can be affected financially. The parent's daughter Beth was diagnosed with various mental disorders and learning disabilities since the third grade and was given an IEP (Individualized Educational Plan) and placed on various medications over the years. While attending an alternative learning school, and after being committed to mental health facilities several times, Beth kicked a filing cabinet at school. She was charged and committed to the Youth Detention Facility in Georgia. Beth also was caught shoplifting a pack of gum, causing the parents to pay $485 and court costs. Additionally, Beth was convicted of stealing school supplies from a store, after which she was ordered to pay $1700 and placed on probation at the cost of $40 per month. Considering Beth was a minor with various mental health issues, the burden of payment fell on her parents. However, once Beth turned seventeen, under Georgia Law her probation was transferred to the adult probation system. The new probation office found no reason, despite the mental health issues of Beth, to keep her two working parents abreast of her court dates and appointments. Thereafter, without the assistance of her parents, Beth fell behind on her obligations and a warrant issued for violation of probation. Also, due to the warrant, Social Security dropped Beth's disability benefits and was seeking reimbursement for benefits paid. When she was arrested on the warrant, the judge in the adult court did not inquire as to her ability to pay, or her parent's ability to pay even though her mother was present in court. Despite Beth's mental health issues and unemployment at the time, the judge sent Beth to jail. A few days later, her parents were able to raise money to get their daughter out of jail. Altogether, they paid approximately $4,000 plus probation fees.[9] According to the report, the parents are still paying the probation fees and reimbursing Social Security at a rate of about $80 per month.

The ACLU report also details a collection effort that Washington State had in place until the State Supreme Court ruled in 2010 that the state's "auto-jail" policies were unconstitutional. In 1999, James Nason received an order to pay $750 in fines after a burglary conviction. Seven years later, he was arrested for failure to pay. At the time of his arrest, he was unemployed, living in his car, and was receiving food stamps as his only source of income. He owed more than double the original debt because of interest. The court ordered Mr. Nason to pay $25 a month toward the fines or to automatically report to jail by a certain date. Under the auto-jail order, if he failed to pay or turn himself in, he would be arrested and jailed without a hearing to determine if the nonpayment was willful. Nason was arrested again and sentenced to 120 days in jail and to pay $30 per month after his release or turn himself into jail for another sixty-day sentence under another auto-jail order. Finally, an attorney on Mr. Nason's behalf successfully appealed the case, and the State Supreme Court found the auto-jail policies violated his due process rights.

The in-depth 2010 report of the American Civil Liberties Union gives a glimpse of case studies conducted throughout the nation. From the report it is clear that the hardest hit by debtors' prisons are without a doubt the poorest people and minorities. The case studies identified surely are clear examples of such. However, what is overlooked by many is the broader impact on society, the first being the cost to the State Government to collect these financial obligations often from people who cannot pay in the first place. There are numerous costs to the state associated with the collection of the late fees, such as the wages to the clerks, sheriffs, attorneys, judges, and probation and correctional officers spent to document the legal financial obligations, track payments, issue warrants, and bring the debtor before the court. When added up in any jurisdiction, the amount of the collection process probably does not exceed the cost to house debtors' in the state prison system. In addition, the increase in the number of people being jailed places an undue burden on the justice system itself. A system that is already overburdened. More debtors imprisoned means more overcrowding at jails, more transports needed to carry people to and from court, and more time judges have to spend on cases that are strictly for the collection of money.

Then there is the cost to society. Going to jail may have various effects on people in different ways. People are separated from family and can't provide their children with basic necessities or emotional support. Their obligations to work will definitely be interfered with. Chances are the debtor was probably already having difficulty with employment to begin with, which got them into the position in which they find themselves. Most likely time from work will be missed, and if debtors have child support obligations on top of the court debt, they may fall behind. If they fall behind on child support, that may cause a chain reaction, and the other parent who is supposed to receive the child support could be affected. If the debtors were to lose their employment, they would be forced to collect unemployment, if they qualify, and state governments do not get employment tax revenue.

Those debtors on probation who owe fines at the completion of their sentence may have their probation extended strictly for financial obligations. Violators may be jailed, causing the state to incur further costs to house these individuals. Probation violations of this type may have other monetary effects on people. Under federal statutes, a probation and parole violator will be unable to collect certain social welfare benefits, such as Food Stamps, SSI benefits, affordable public housing, and Welfare.[10] This, in turn, can cause a desperate individual to potentially commit further crimes.

Strides have been made across the country to reform the process of court debt collection. The Brennan Center for Justice identified the smallest state in the union, Rhode Island, as a success story in the criminal justice debt collection practices.[11] The Brennan Center report gives honors to the social organization Rhode Island Family Law Center for undertaking a comprehensive study of court debt in Rhode Island for three years prior to 2008. The Family Law Center found that court debt was the most common reason people were jailed in Rhode Island.[12] It amounted to 18 percent of all jailing, and the average debt was $826.[13] In many cases, the State was spending more on incarcerating the debtors than what was being collected or even the total debt owed. Therefore, in 2008, the Rhode Island Family Law Center and other social organizations lobbied the Rhode Island State Legislature to pass reforms in this area. The Legislature passed the reforms designed to protect low-income court debtors. First, policymakers reduced the length of debt-related jail time by requiring the Court to hold an ability-to-pay hearing promptly after a debtor's arrest. Now, debtors arrested during judicial business hours are required to be taken directly to court for a hearing, and all others must be seen within forty-eight hours.[14] Second, the legislature attempted to reduce the size of the debtor inmate population through the introduction of a systematic assessment tool for ability-to-pay determinations and a subsequent cost abatement allowance for defendants who qualify as indigent. The State statute mandates that judges and magistrates systematically assess defendants' ability to pay using a "standardized . . . financial assessment instrument" that inquires into defendants' receipt of welfare benefits and their other outstanding debt obligations, including child support and restitution.[15] Determinations of ability-to-pay must take place first "immediately after sentencing or nearly thereafter as practicable" and again after a defendant is arrested for debt delinquency.[16] Judges and magistrates are then authorized to abate the costs of any defendant who legally qualifies as "unable to pay" under statutory guidelines.[17]

As one of the authors of this book and a member of the Rhode Island State Senate at the time the 2008 legislative reforms were considered and approved, it is a great pleasure to announce that the reforms have worked in the State. Not only was I member of the Senate at the time, but I also sat on the Senate Judiciary Committee that held hearings on the issue and later approved the issue for a full Senate vote. Looking at the effect the reforms made, in 2015, approximately 1,556 adults were arrested and committed to the Rhode Island Intake Detention Center solely for failure to appear at a court payment date. Debtors thus comprised 15.5 percent of the total inmate population in 2015. Arrested debtors owed an average of $1,082 upon commitment, and they were predominantly low-income and nonviolent misdemeanor offenders with a mixed history of debt payment compliance. At least half of arrested debtors had no consistent source of income available to make debt payments—45 percent were unemployed, 52 percent received food stamps, and 5 percent received Social Security benefits. Three-fourths of arrested debtors were misdemeanor offenders—one-third were originally sentenced for "driving with a suspended license." Perhaps because of the low-income status of this population, most debtors arrested in 2015 had a history of trying and failing to comply with court debt obligations. A majority of arrested debtors had made one or more prior payments on the case on which they ultimately received a bench warrant—but 86 percent had received at least one bench warrant for failure to appear in the past, and 58 percent had previously experienced debt-related incarceration. A look at the implementation of court debt reforms reveals that the Rhode Island Department of Corrections and the Judiciary have effectively worked together to limit jail time to forty-eight hours for the vast majority of arrested debtors. Arrested debtors in 2015 were held for an average of 1.21 nights in jail, and 87.5 percent of the debtor inmate population saw a judge or magistrate within two days. This successful implementation of the measures in State Law represents a significant improvement from 2007, when the average arrested debtor was held in jail for three nights before seeing a judge. Despite these impressive efficiency gains in the hearing process, approximately 30 percent of arrested debtors in 2015 were subsequently incarcerated *after* seeing a judge in court. As seen in our discussion involving *Bearden v. Georgia*, this pattern of posthearing incarceration prevents further reductions in Rhode Island's inmate population, and it may also be unlawful. As we know, courts are not allowed to incarcerate delinquent debtors unless they formally establish that their failure to pay debts was "willful" per Our Supreme Court in *Bearden v. Georgia*.

If we look at the assessment of ability-to-pay and cost abatement, we find the debtor inmate population has fallen by 14 percent since 2007, but the judiciary's limited use of cost abatement for eligible debtors represents a missed opportunity to protect indigent debtors and further reduce the inmate population. The judiciary has not adopted a financial assessment instrument for use during ability-to-pay determinations that include the criteria in State Law. While clerks and magistrates consistently inquire into arrested debtors' employment status and occasionally probe for other details about their lives (for example, their housing situation), they rarely ask for information pertaining to public benefits receipt or the presence of other debt obligations. Perhaps due to limited use of the legislature's ability-to-pay criteria, magistrates abated the costs of just 3 percent of arrested debtors in 2015. The fact that roughly half of the arrested debtors in 2015 received food stamps indicates that magistrates do not exercise their authority to abate court costs for a majority of those who are eligible.

Rhode Island also has a similar statute to Ohio in that a debtor can pay down their outstanding court fines and costs for each day of incarceration.[18] Prior to 2012, the Rhode Island law gave the debtor a credit of $150 per day. In 2012, the state legislature reduced the credit to $50 per day. As a practicing lawyer in the State of Rhode Island, I am told the change in law was due to the increasing number of debtors showing up to court requesting to be sent to jail to work off the debt. Under the old law at $150 per day, a person could get a set of over a thousand dollars in fines in one week. More than what some people make in a week. Then add in the cost to the State to house these individuals while they choose to go to jail for their debt. At the rate of $50 per day, people are less likely to use the law as a debt reduction tool.

In a short perusal through magazines, newspapers, and online articles, one will find numerous articles about the rise of debtors' prisons in America. However, most, if not all, of those articles will have a central theme: Poverty and Race. While the authors recognize the fact that debtors' prisons reported throughout this country largely affect low-income people and minorities, the purpose of this book is to bring to light that anyone can face debtors' prison square in the face. Some may not go to actual prison, but only because they have the money to stay out. But staying out can cost individuals and their families dearly. Take the case of Lori, a retired school teacher from Henrico County, Virginia. Lori has spent her retirement funds keeping her adult son out of prison. Her son, who battles alcoholism and mental illness, had a run-in with the law for a larceny charge. He was placed on probation and ordered to pay $300 in restitution to the store but was then slapped with $1,700 in court fees. Additionally, because the court felt his troubles stem from his alcoholism, Lori's son has been on a SCRAM bracelet to the tune of $300 per month. A SCRAM bracelet continually monitors the blood alcohol in a person's body. All the while, her son's only income is $500 per month he receives from Social Security Disability. The mother, who never would consider herself a low-income individual and worked her whole life as a teacher, is now struggling because she pays the bill to keep her son out of prison. Lori never went to prison and neither did her son, but she lives in her own debtors' prison like thousands of other Americans.

While you may think "this will never happen to me," think again. Alexandria, a single parent working as an RN in Orange County, California, never thought so. Until her child riding in the back of her car one day decided to unbuckle herself to wave to the nice police officer traveling behind them.

The same nice police officer pulled Alexandria over and wrote her a $300 moving violation. She forgot to pay the ticket, and after a number of years the ticket grew close to $5,000. A warrant was issued, and police were called to her apartment complex for an unrelated matter. The police asked for identification from all parties present, and Alex was arrested on the outstanding warrant. At the time, she was having medical problems and was scheduled for surgery, but the warrant had priority. She spent two days in jail before she was released due to overcrowding in the California jails and placed on a payment plan to pay off her $5,000 ticket.

Debtors' prisons are not limited to criminal justice debt. In fact, a February 2018 report from the ACLU titled "A Pound of Flesh: The Criminalization of Private Debt" is the result of a yearlong study of thousands of debtors who owe private commercial debt being jailed each year throughout this country, and millions more threatened with jail.[19] The debts can be any type of consumer bill, including medical bills. In 2011, for example, Robin Sanders of Illinois was driving home when an officer pulled her over for having a loud muffler. Instead of being sent off with a warning, the officer arrested Sanders and took her to jail. This was when she found out that she had a warrant against her for failing to appear in a Macoupin County court for an unpaid $730 medical bill. Unbeknownst to Sanders, a collection agency had filed a lawsuit against her, and, having never received the notice instructing her to appear, she had missed her date in court. She spent four days in jail waiting for her father to raise $500 for her bail. That money was then turned over to the collection agency.

Unpaid student loans, credit cards bills, mortgages, and car payments can also cost you your freedom, and it can be over as little as a few dollars. As the ACLU put it, it is the silent financial crisis, and it can happen to you.

10

IF IT'S BROKE, DON'T FIX IT

OUR CRIMINAL JUSTICE system is clearly broken, as it focuses far too much on overcriminalization and incarceration instead of justice, which is a practice that is exceedingly dangerous to the middle class, in particular, as this chapter will bear out.

There is increasing talk about reforms to both the criminal justice and correctional systems, but so far not much has been done. Our country can talk about reforms, yet it is no guarantee that these reforms will ever happen. The main reason may be that government budgets continue to rely more heavily on fines and fees from the criminal justice system to balance their budgets. For instance, Texas refuses to get rid of the ten-year-old practice that suspends driver's licenses and sends people to jail. The scheme exists for the sole purpose of racking up fees on people caught driving under the influence, without insurance or without a license. Calls to scrap the program are controversial, and a recent Senate report stated that prohibiting the program is not plausible in light of budget constraints. In other words, it is too lucrative, raising $65 million a year by tacking on surcharges to fines, fees and court costs paid by motorists for various traffic offenses.[1] Those who do not pay forfeit their driver's licenses. Texas cannot change the law because they cannot replace the lost revenue. Additionally, the correctional officers' unions won't favor the reforms that call for reduced prison population for fear of its members losing their jobs. How can a system hope to reduce prison population when their jobs depend on the population for job security? There are some American towns, once dependent on farming, mining, and manufacturing, that are now wholly dependent on a prison. So while the reforms all sound like great ideas, in actuality it is all just political rhetoric.

NO ESCAPE FROM DEBT

Consolidated Credit, a debt consolidation company, runs a commercial advertising their services in which debt is depicted as a green, black-caped vampire bat. Their slogan is "Don't let credit card debt suck the life out of you." The color is certainly symbolic, and the analogy is accurate as your financial resources and your economic lifeblood are slowly being drained away.

Americans today continue to be sent to jail not for committing a crime, but because they cannot afford to pay for bills that include traffic tickets, medical care, and court fees. If that sounds a lot like a debtors' prison, that's because it is. Although debtors' prisons are unconstitutional, working class people are routinely imprisoned for their inability to pay fines, and courts and judges in states across the land are violating the Constitution by allowing this practice to go on.

Roughly a third of US states today jail people for not paying off their debts, from court-related fines and fees to credit card and car loans, a practice that contravenes a 1983 United States Supreme Court ruling that they violate the Constitution's Equal Protection Clause. Some states apply late fees, payment plan fees, and interest when people are unable to pay all their debts at once. Alabama charges a 30 percent collection fee, for instance, while Florida allows private debt collectors to add a 40 percent surcharge on the original debt. Some Florida counties also use so-called collection courts, where debtors can be jailed but have no right to a public defender. In North Carolina, people are charged for using a public defender, and it is not only poor defendants who are unable to afford such costs and are forced to forgo legal counsel.[2] More and more hardworking, middle-class Americans are being sucked into this black hole of expanding debt from which they cannot escape.

The high rates of unemployment and government fiscal shortfalls that followed the housing crash have increased the use of debtors' prisons, as states look for ways to replenish their coffers. Cash-strapped cities and states are increasingly trying to tap a previously overlooked pot of money—uncollected fines, fees, and other costs imposed by civil and criminal courts—in order to help them balance their books. And when people don't pay these court-ordered debts, some local officials have not been shy about tossing them in jail, leading to the creation of modern-day debtors' prisons. While there are no comprehensive data on how many states jail citizens for court-related debt, several organizations, including the Brennan Center, have raised alarms over what they say is the widespread practice of locking up poor offenders in violation of federal law, citing Supreme Court rulings that someone can only be incarcerated for "willfully" refusing to pay.[3]

James Robert Nason could be a case study for the court-debt-prison cycle when, in 1999, he pleaded guilty to second-degree burglary in Spokane, Washington. He was sentenced to thirty days in jail and community service and was ordered to pay $735 in court costs, attorney fees, and restitution. That debt began to accrue 12 percent annual interest from the day of his sentencing. Nason didn't finish the community service and didn't keep up with the payments. As a result, he served more than 120 days behind bars over several years, despite arguing that he couldn't afford to pay. At one hearing, he said he was both homeless and unemployed. In 2006, as he faced 120 more days in jail, his court-appointed appellate lawyer argued that Spokane's self-described "auto jail," which put Nason behind bars without a hearing whenever he failed to pay, violated his rights to due process.[4]

In 2010, the Washington State Supreme Court agreed. Before imposing sanctions for failure to pay court debt, "a trial court must inquire into the offender's ability to pay," the court wrote in its decision in Nason's case. Spokane court officials declined to comment, citing pending lawsuits. Certain counties in Florida, Ohio, Georgia, and elsewhere also routinely imprison people who fail to keep up with court debt, according to the American Civil Liberties Union and the Brennan Center. In practice, advocates said, courts often fail to inquire about a defendant's ability to pay until after they're incarcerated. Even states that do not regularly jail debtors may use the threat of jail to go after fees and fines, with consequences that can play out for years.[5]

Nora Gonzalez, a forty-year-old Seattle resident, discovered how persistent court-ordered debt could be after she was convicted in 2005 of passing a bad check. She served a few days in jail at the time and was sentenced to make payments to the court. Last year, she found she owed more than $3,000 in restitution, which has now gone to collections. She must pay her outstanding fines and fees, then wait five years before she can have her record expunged and become relicensed in her former occupation as a caregiver. Without a job, she struggles to pay them. But until she pays them, she cannot work. In what critics see as an example of collection efforts run amok, Philadelphia in 2010 began to collect court-related debt dating to 1971, after a series in the *Philadelphia Inquirer* revealed the city had failed to collect an estimated $1.5 billion. A review by the courts determined that an estimated 400,000 residents owed the city money—cash that Philadelphia, facing a $1.35 billion budget shortfall over five years, sorely needs. First Judicial District President Judge Pamela Dembe defended the program, which critics say has been problematic because of often incomplete payment information, making it difficult—and in some cases impossible—to prove whether the debt has been paid.[6]

In 2006, Tyeisha Gamble, twenty-six, who lives on Philadelphia's north side with her two-year-old son and her boyfriend, was convicted of simple assault, a misdemeanor, after an altercation with a coworker. Included in her criminal conviction—her first and only—was about $500 in court-ordered fees and fines. She said she did her best to pay her debt while attending school, racking up more debt with student loans, but fell behind. In 2011, she earned her BA in fashion marketing from the Philadelphia Institute of

Art. But Gamble said her criminal record, which can't be expunged unless she pays her debt, has made it nearly impossible to land a job in her field. Compounding the problem, in Pennsylvania, as in most states, criminal justice debt can also lead to civil penalties, including suspension of driver's licenses, garnishment of wages, and loss of public benefits.[7]

The practice of imprisoning people for debt is obviously being fueled by economic woes that have decimated many state and city budgets. But debtors' prisons are also on the rise thanks to the zeal of private companies that file lawsuits against debtors and often "fail to serve them with notice of court dates or intentionally serve them at incorrect addresses," as the Brennan Center for Justice's Inimai Chettiar noted. "When debtors do not show up, agencies procure arrest warrants from courts, leading to incarceration of the debtors. Bail is usually set at an amount equal to or higher than the original fees and fines they defendants couldn't pay in the first place. All this has amounted to a return of debtors' prisons.,"Chettiar concluded.[8]

The overabundance of vague laws only makes matters worse, rendering otherwise innocent activities illegal. As a result, today we find ourselves operating in a strange new world where farmers who dare to make unpasteurized goat cheese and share it with members of their community are finding their farms raided, while home gardeners face jail time for daring to cultivate their own varieties of orchids without having completed sufficient paperwork.[9]

In 2012, George Will wrote about a marine biologist, Nancy Black, who was charged with a crime of feeding killer whales. Seven years earlier, as part of a National Oceanographic and Atmospheric Institute study of the feeding habit of killer whales, Nancy and other crew members were filming the killer whales feeding on the carcass of a gray whale that the killer whales had killed. Nancy went from being featured on PBS, Animal Planet, and National Geographic to admitting to one misdemeanor violation of the Marine Mammal Protection Act. As part of her sentence and plea agreement, the federal government placed her on three years probation, ordered her to perform 300 hours of community service and pay a $12,500 fine, and ordered her to stay 100 yards away from whales. Originally, the government had charged her with crimes that called for a twenty-seven-year prison sentence and $700,000 in fines. All for feeding orcas food they killed in the first place, as part of the circle of life.

In an editorial, Will wrote that such laws, "which enable government zealots to accuse almost anyone of committing three felonies in a day, do not just enable government misconduct, they incite prosecutors to intimidate decent people who never had culpable intentions. And to inflict punishments without crimes."[10]

This frightening state of affairs, where a person can actually be arrested and incarcerated for the most innocent and inane activities—including digging up arrowheads, abandoning a snowmobile in a snowstorm, collecting rainwater on one's own property, and feeding a whale—is due to what law scholars refer to as overcriminalization, or the overt proliferation of criminal laws. Black spent her life savings defending herself, money that she could have been better spent elsewhere, for both sides. The government likely spent millions bringing the charges.

Will wrote, "Often, as in Black's case, they are untethered from the common law tradition of *mens rea*, which holds that a crime must involve a criminal intent—a guilty mind. Legions of government lawyers inundate targets like Black with discovery demands, producing financial burdens that compel the innocent to surrender in order to survive."[11]

Excessive, confusing statutes cost money, wreck the lives of upstanding citizens, and discourage economic growth.

SCHOOLS OR PRISONS?

According to 2016 brief from the US Department of Education, over the past three decades, state and local government expenditures on prisons and jails have increased about three times as fast as spending on elementary and secondary education. At the postsecondary level, the contrast is even starker. From 1989 to 2013, state and local spending on corrections rose by

89 percent, while state and local appropriations for higher education remained flat. This increase in corrections spending has been driven by, among other factors, an increase in the number of people incarcerated in prisons and jails. The Department of Education brief highlighted several linkages that exist between educational attainment and incarceration. For example, two-thirds of state prison inmates have not completed high school. Young black men between the ages of twenty and twenty-four who do not have a high school diploma (or an equivalent credential) have a greater chance of being incarcerated than of being employed. At the same time, researchers have estimated that a 10 percent increase in high school graduation rates may result in a 9 percent decline in criminal arrest rates.[12]

In 2016, the *Washington Post* reported on the US Department of Education's findings. The analysis underscored the growing bipartisan agreement about the need for criminal justice reform and the argument that taxpayers and public safety would be better served by redirecting investments from incarceration to public schools. A variety of studies have suggested that investing more in education, particularly targeted toward at-risk communities, could achieve crime reduction without the heavy social costs that high incarceration rates impose on individuals, families, and communities.[13]

According to Education Secretary John B. King Jr., these findings should give us all a reason to pause and provide a lens through which we can examine our values as communities and as a country. King's predecessor, Arne Duncan, called on states and cities to dramatically reduce incarceration for nonviolent crimes and use the estimated $15 billion in savings to substantially raise teacher pay in high-poverty schools. With a move like this, Duncan believes we'd not just make a bet on education over incarceration, we'd signal the beginning of a long-range effort to pay our nation's teachers what they are worth. That sort of investment wouldn't just make teachers and struggling communities feel more valued. It would have ripple effects on our economy and on our civic life.[14]

The report described wide variation in spending on prisons and schools among the states: Total corrections spending grew 149 percent in

Massachusetts, for example, compared with 850 percent in Texas. Total education spending rose from 18 percent in Michigan to 326 percent in Nevada. Even taking population and enrollment changes into account, there were striking disparities in the rate of spending increases. The rate of increase in per capita corrections spending outpaced the rate of increase in per pupil education spending in every state but two, Massachusetts and New Hampshire. In twenty-three states, per capita spending rose more than twice as fast as per pupil spending.[15]

The White House Council of Economic Advisers released a report at that time concluding that a greater investment in education and raising the minimum wage are much more effective ways to protect the public than spending $80 billion a year on incarceration. With over 2.2 million people behind bars across the nation, and about 70 million Americans who have a criminal record that can make it difficult to get a job, vote, or otherwise participate in society,[16] mass incarceration is not good for our country. Nor does it make us safer.

PAYBACK

In April 2017, The Supreme Court ruled that Colorado's practice of not automatically refunding court fees and other costs to people convicted of crimes but later exonerated violates the Constitution. The 7-1 decision sided with two people, Nelson and Madden, whose convictions for sexual offenses were later thrown out. One paid about $700 in court fees, including victim restitution, while the other paid more than $4,400 in similar costs. Colorado law had required people cleared of wrongdoing to recover their costs in a separate civil lawsuit. But they could not get a refund unless they proved their innocence by clear and convincing evidence.[17]

Justice Ruth Bader Ginsburg said those hurdles violated the due process rights of criminal defendants, citing that the state may not retain their money simply because their convictions were in place when the funds were taken, for once those convictions were erased, the presumption of Nelson's and Madden's innocence was restored.

Colorado appeared to be the only state that didn't automatically refund such fees. Justice Samuel Alito wrote separately to say that that the majority went too far in saying that an award of victim restitution should always be returned when a defendant's conviction is reversed. Justice Clarence Thomas dissented, saying the defendants did not have a constitutional right to recover costs and fees they paid to the state. Justice Neil Gorsuch did not take part in the US Supreme Court case, which was argued before he took his seat on the Court. Spurred by the Supreme Court case, Colorado's Legislature passed a bill giving those exonerated a refund of court costs and other fees without having to prove their innocence again. Gov. John Hickenlooper signed the bill into law in March 2017. The measure was supported by Colorado Attorney General Cynthia Coffman, who defended the state before the Supreme Court. A second measure signed into law that same year allowed people found innocent of felony crimes after serving time in jail or prison to receive a lump sum compensation payment in lieu of annual payments. Those exonerated are eligible to receive $70,000 per year incarcerated and $25,000 per year spent on parole.[18]

These bills are, at least, the start of some of the many prison reforms that are so long overdue.

DEBTORS' PRISON REFORM

Nearly two centuries ago, the United States formally abolished the incarceration of people who failed to pay off debts. However, recent years have witnessed the rise of modern-day debtors' prisons—the arrest and jailing of poor people for failure to pay legal debts they can never hope to afford, through criminal justice procedures that violate their most basic rights.

State and local courts have increasingly attempted to supplement their funding by charging fees to people convicted of crimes, including fees for public defenders, prosecutors, court administration, jail operation, and probation supervision. And in the face of mounting budget deficits at the state and local level, courts across the country have used aggressive tactics to collect these unpaid fines and fees, including for traffic offenses and other low-level offenses. These courts have ordered the arrest and jailing of people who fall behind on their payments, without affording any hearings to determine an individual's ability to pay or offering alternatives to payment such as community service.[19]

In response, since 2009, the ACLU and ACLU affiliates across the country have been exposing and challenging modern-day debtors' prisons and urging governments and courts to pursue more rational and equitable approaches to criminal justice debt. Debtors' prisons impose devastating human costs. They lead to coercive debt collection, forcing poor people to forgo the basic necessities of life in order to avoid arrest and jailing. Debtors' prisons waste taxpayer money and resources by jailing people who may never be able to pay their debts. The practice imposes direct costs on the government and further destabilizes the lives of poor people struggling to pay their debts and leave the criminal justice system behind. And most troubling, debtors' prisons create a racially-skewed, two-tiered system of justice in which the poor receive harsher, longer punishments for committing the same crimes as the rich, simply because they are poor. Ultimately, debtors' prisons are not only unfair and insensible, but they are also illegal. Imprisoning someone because he or she cannot afford to pay court-imposed fines or fees violates the Fourteenth Amendment promises of due process and equal protection under the law. The ACLU and ACLU affiliates are uncovering how debtors' prisons across the country undermine the criminal justice system and threaten civil rights and civil liberties. They are continuing to work in state legislatures and courts, and with judicial officials, to end these practices once and for all.[20]

11

DEBT AND THE WHITE HOUSE

WE HEAR SO much about debt these days: individual debt, family debt, even cities and towns that owe so much they run out of money and become functionally bankrupt. The US government is no exception. Many of us have heard the almost incalculable number twenty-trillion dollars that is our national debt presently, and getting larger every day.

How can the government get away with it, not paying what they own, and instead, borrowing more and more money in order to keep functioning? It's a fair question, and worthy of an answer. However, the question is a bit more complex than it might seem. In some ways, the government is like every ordinary American family. It has a bank account. Every day the funds in that account grow by the amount of deposits that are made and shrink by the amount of withdrawals.[1]

There is a lot of money coming into and going from America's bank account, and the bottom line is that how quickly it changes can be dizzying. Good luck balancing *that* checkbook.

Deposits come from tax receipts, air transport security fees, the postal service, Medicare premiums, and earnings from the Federal Reserve itself. Withdrawals go to pay for everything the government does: federal employee salaries, income tax refunds, NASA, interest on our debt, unemployment insurance benefits, and paying defense contracts. A big source of deposits for the government is usually the government selling bonds. And that's where the debt ceiling comes in: if the government cannot sell any more bonds because it's hit the debt ceiling, it won't have the funds to pay for all those things for which it makes withdrawals. That includes Social Security checks and interest payments on the debt. When the government writes a check, it goes to whoever is getting paid. The payee then deposits it in its own bank account. The bank then submits it to the Federal Reserve for clearing. So far, that's pretty much the same thing that happens when anyone else writes a check. Millions of Americans have overdraft protection on checking accounts that allows them to write checks in excess of the amounts deposited in the accounts. This is sometimes controversial, because banks often attach high fees to overdrafts, which means that you could put a $3 cup of coffee on your debit card and get hit with a $35 fee. But those kinds of fees are generally waived for very wealthy bank customers who, ironically, enjoy feeless overdrafts. The United States almost certainly enjoys unlimited overdraft protection from the Federal Reserve, because there is almost zero chance the Federal Reserve would ever bounce a check written by the US government.[2]

Think about it. The check comes into the Federal Reserve. It looks at the US government balance and discovers that we're at zero. What does the Federal Reserve do? I'm pretty sure the Federal Reserve would go ahead and credit the bank submitting the check with the deposit to account for the fund transfer. Legally, this is a bit murky. It's not clear that the Federal Reserve would be required to clear a check that exceeded the amount on deposit. It may be within its authority to reject the check. But rejecting a check written by the government of the United States would probably violate the dual mandate of the Fed to pursue maximum employment and price stability. A US government that bounced checks would introduce so much chaos, the Fed would likely be obligated by its core mandates to credit the check.[3] Without getting into the intricacies of debt ceiling violation, and what can occur when the amount of money the government borrows reaches its upper limit, suffice it to say that the Treasury cannot actually run out of money. It can only run out if it decides to stop writing checks sufficient to pay all of our obligations.[4]

A BRIEF HISTORY OF AMERICAN DEBT

Government debt might be as old as the founding of the original colonies, but its growth has been steady, and never has it been as high as it is at this moment in time. Wars, in particular, have always been financed.

Many people might be aware of some of the factors pertaining to the issues of our nation's incremental debt increases between the Ronald Reagan and Bill Clinton administrations, before nearly doubling during the presidential term of George W. Bush, reaching $10 trillion, and then doubling again during the presidency of Barack Obama. The history of this country's debt goes much further.

During the conflict, Congress could not finance the Revolutionary War with large tax raises, as the memory of unjust taxation from the British stood fresh in the minds of the American public. Instead, the Continental Congress (made up of delegates from the Thirteen Colonies) borrowed money from other nations. The founders led negotiations, with Benjamin Franklin securing loans of over $2 million from the French Government and President John Adams obtaining a loan from Dutch bankers. We also borrowed from domestic creditors. While the war was still going on, in 1781, Congress established the US Department of Finance. Two years later, as the war ended in 1783, the Department of Finance reported US debt to the American Public for the first time. Congress took initiative to raise taxes then, as the total debt reached $43 million.[5]

The War of 1812 more than doubled the nation's debt. It increased from $45.2 million to $119.2 million by September 1815. The Treasury Department issued bonds to pay a portion of the debt, but it was not until Andrew Jackson became president and determined to master the debt that this "national curse," as he deemed it, was addressed. By selling federally owned western lands and blocking spending on infrastructure projects, Jackson paid off the national debt after six years in office. This actually created a government surplus that Jackson divided among indebted states. When President Jackson shrank that debt to zero in 1835, it was the only time in US history when the country was free of debt. The time of prosperity was short-lived, as state banks began printing money and offering easy credit, and land value dropped.[6]

The Civil War (1861–1865) alone is estimated to have cost $5.2 billion by its end, and government debt skyrocketed from $65 million to $2.6 billion. Post-Civil War inflation, along with economic disturbance from Europe's financial struggles, contributed to the vulnerable economic climate of the late 19th century. The collapse of Jay Cooke & Co., a major bank invested in railroading, caused the Panic of 1873. Nearly a quarter of the country's railroads went bankrupt, more than 18,000 businesses closed, unemployment hit 14 percent, and the New York Stock Exchange began sinking. This period of deflation and low growth continued for sixty-five months, making it the longest depression, according to the National Bureau of Economic Research. During this time, the government collected less money in taxes, and the national debt grew.[7]

People started investing heavily in the stock market in 1920, unaware that Black Tuesday would dawn with an $8 billion loss in market value when the stock market crashed on October 29, 1929. The United States relied on the gold standard and raised inflation, rather than lowering rates to ease the burden of inflation. During the following era, income inequality between classes grew. More than 25 percent of the workforce was unemployed, and people made purchases on credit and were forced into foreclosures and repossessions. President Franklin D. Roosevelt developed programs for unemployment pay and social security pensions and provided assistance to labor unions. Although Roosevelt addressed many problems in the US economy, the funding for his programs grew the national debt to $33 billion. During World War II (1939 to 1945), the US lent Britain and other countries money to help pay for military costs and spent a great deal for their own military. By the end of that war, US debt reached $285 billion. Following the war, the US economy grew, but the trend of a postwar reduction of national debt did not continue. Within a few decades, the Vietnam War and programs to help the poor, fund education, and improve transportation increased debt further. By the end of the Ronald Reagan era, the national debt was $2.7 trillion. The Presidency of Bill Clinton was marked with tax increases, reductions in defense spending, and an economic boom that reduced the growth of debt, but it still reached a staggering $5.6 trillion by 2000. The increase in federal debt between 1990 and 2000 was minimal when considering how it more than doubled in 2010 to $13.5 trillion. Today, it has surpassed 20 trillion.[8]

Most headlines focus on how much the United States owes China, one of the largest foreign owners. What many people don't know is that the Social Security Trust Fund, a.k.a. *your* retirement money, owns most of the national debt.[9]

So, with the approximate 350 million Americans responsible for $20 trillion in debt, could China put us all in debtors' prison? Might Trump's wall be extended around the perimeter of the entire country to punish everyone for not paying China what we owe them?

It's interesting to think about, especially after so many examples of individuals being jailed over some very meager fines and bills they could not pay back.

REAL CHANGE STARTS AT THE TOP

Debtors' prisons—relics of the past that were outlawed two centuries ago in America—impose devastating human costs, as we have previously described. In 2015, the Obama Justice Department issued a 185-page report in its investigation of the Ferguson Police Department in Missouri, following the police shooting of teenager Michael Brown. The report exposed how

Ferguson police sought to advance the "City's focus on revenue rather than . . . public safety needs," leading to the routine jailing of poor people to elicit court fine and fee payments.[10]

Ironically, the judge who most frequently sent Ferguson residents to over-crowded prisons for their petty fines not only personally benefited from the system—he moonlighted as both a prosecutor and a private attorney when he was not sitting on the bench—but also owed more than $170,000 in unpaid taxes. A 2014 *Washington Post* investigation found that some towns in Missouri derived 40 percent or more of their annual revenue from the hefty fines and fees collected by municipal courts.[11]

One of the duties of the US Justice Department, a federal executive department of the US government, is to run the federal prison system. The position of attorney general was created by the Judiciary Act of 1789. In June 1870, Congress enacted a law titled "An Act to Establish the Department of Justice." This Act established the attorney general as head of the Department of Justice and gave the attorney general direction and control of US attorneys and all other counsel employed on behalf of the United States. The Act also vested in the attorney general supervisory power over the accounts of US attorneys and US marshals. The mission of the Office of the attorney general is to supervise and direct the administration and operation of the Depart-ment of Justice, including the Federal Bureau of Investigation; the Drug Enforcement Administration; the Bureau of Alcohol, Tobacco, Firearms, and Explosives; the Bureau of Prisons; the Office of Justice Programs; and the US Attorneys and US Marshals Service, which are all within the Depart-ment of Justice.[12]

The Department of Justice and the office of attorney general serve all Americans and are not supposed to be partisan and political in any way. When it comes to prison reform, it is something that has been talked about for a long time, and through numerous presidential administrations. It is a topic that seems to be gaining some traction as of late, however. Even if it does not appear that a lot has been done with regard to real prison reform when it comes to debt in particular, we at least hear about it more and more. And that is a start.

On Dec. 2, 2015, the Justice Department hosted a convening to address the effect and fairness of fees and fines. The Department convened judges, academics, and practitioners to develop a research and policy agenda that will inform jurisdictions in their efforts to reform court practices. On Dec. 3, the White House and the Department cosponsored an event called "A Cycle of Incarceration: Prison, Debt and Bail Practices," to bring public attention to the connection between poverty and the criminal justice system and highlight state reform efforts. The White House Council of Economic Advisers also released an issue brief exploring the economic inefficiency of fines, fees, and bail and their disproportionate impact on the poor.

In this letter released by the Justice Department in the final year of the Obama Administration, the DOJ expressed a commitment to fairness in the criminal justice system on several fronts:

- Criminal justice reform is a top priority for the administration and specifically for the Justice Department. The department has taken significant steps to prevent vulnerable communities from becoming justice-involved, and to promote initiatives that reduce the likelihood of recidivism.
- The department's efforts also include addressing problems that obstruct opportunity, such as poverty, since those who are economically disadvantaged are more easily caught up in the criminal justice system and face greater barriers to reentry. Among these efforts are numerous diversion and reentry programs, as well as the White House Legal Aid Interagency Roundtable, which works to improve federal anti-poverty programs by providing access to legal aid.

- The department is particularly concerned about criminal justice system practices that perpetuate and exacerbate poverty by imposing unnecessary and exorbitant fees and fines, unjust collection practices, unwarranted suspension of drivers' licenses and other legal obligations. Such penalties may appear small in isolation, but in the obligations can easily and rapidly add up.

- These and other practices are not only unwise and harmful, but also inconsistent with constitutional mandates. For example, people are routinely assessed fines that they cannot afford and then jailed for nonpayment without any inquiry into their ability to pay, as required by the Constitution.

- These harms are most frequently felt by the most vulnerable members of our communities, and often in cases involving minor offenses, such as traffic citations. Fees and fines have significant consequences. Individuals face repeated, unnecessary incarceration in already overcrowded jails, lose their jobs and their housing, face escalating debt and often become trapped in cycles of poverty that can be nearly impossible to escape.[13]

In the DOJ letter, The Council of Economic Advisers issued a brief that touched firmly on the issue of sentencing people to prison over debt:

- Increasing Use of Fines, Fees and Bail: As higher levels of incarceration and law enforcement have placed budgetary pressure on states and local governments, they have increasingly turned to criminal justice payments as a source of additional revenue. Available data suggests that about two-thirds of all prison inmates have criminal justice debts, and rising use of bail payments has contributed to a 60 percent increase in the number of un-convicted inmates in jails between 1996 and 2014.

- Disproportionate Impact on the Poor: Because fines and fees do not take into account the defendants' ability to pay, they place a disproportionate burden on lower-income defendants and create a highly regressive system of raising revenue and paying for criminal justice operations. Low-income individuals with criminal justice debts may face difficult tradeoffs between paying their debt and purchasing other necessities, and those unable to pay can face incarceration, demonstrating the large human cost of these policies as well. Bail payments set without consideration of financial circumstances can also result in detaining the poorest defendants rather than the most dangerous. For example, in New York City in 2010, nearly 80 percent of arrestees failed to make bail at arraignment for bail amounts less than $500.

- Economic Inefficiency: Assigning fines and fees to low-income offenders represents a highly inefficient way to raise revenue, as these individuals likely do not have the means to pay. Some states are able to collect less than 20 percent of some types of fees, and the low rate of collection sometimes means that the cost of operating the program exceeds the revenue collected. Incarcerating individuals for failure to pay only furthers this problem, with the cost of incarceration alone sometimes exceeding the debt owed.[14]

What all this translates to is that the Justice Department is asking local courts across the country to be wary of how they slap poor defendants with fines and fees to fill their jurisdictions' coffers, warning that such practices often run afoul of the US Constitution and have serious real-world consequences.[15]

This was news that many people wanted to hear for a long time. But would it translate into something actionable?

In a subsequent letter that was sent to the chief judges and court administrators in all fifty states, Vanita Gupta, the head of the Department's Civil Rights Division, and Lisa Foster, director of the Office for Access to Justice, wrote that illegal enforcement of fines and fees had been receiving increased attention in recent years and that the Justice Department had a "strong interest" in making sure the rights of citizens were protected. The letter detailed seven principles that Gupta and Foster say court personnel should be aware of when imposing fines and fees. The officials wrote that courts should not jail people for nonpayment of fines and fees without first determining whether the nonpayer was indigent and then establishing that the failure to pay was "willful." They wrote that "courts should consider alternatives to jail for indigent defendants; they must not use arrest warrants or license suspensions to coerce payments without giving defendants their rightful constitutional protections, and they must not use bail practices that leave poor people jailed solely because they cannot afford to pay for their release." The officials wrote that courts should not require prepayment as a condition for a judicial hearing; they must provide meaningful notice and—in some cases—lawyers for those facing fines and fees; and they must "safeguard against unconstitutional practices by court staff and private contractors," who are often left enforcing fines and fees because judges devote only a few hours to it on their crowded dockets.[16]

"Individuals may confront escalating debt; face repeated, unnecessary incarceration for nonpayment despite posing no danger to the community; lose their jobs; and become trapped in cycles of poverty that can be nearly impossible to escape," Gupta and Foster wrote. "Furthermore, in addition to being unlawful, to the extent that these practices are geared not toward addressing public safety, but rather toward raising revenue, they can cast doubt on the impartiality of the tribunal and erode trust between local governments and their constituents."[17]

Chiraag Bains, former senior counsel in the DOJ's Civil Rights Division, wrote that the guidance helped jump-start reform around the country. Indeed, there's a strong national movement to eliminate court practices that punish the poor unfairly. The Southern Poverty Law Center in recent years, for example, has scored numerous legal victories that closed debtors' prisons in Alabama and Louisiana and stopped practices that amounted to the unconstitutional extortion of payments to private probation companies as well as city courts.[18]

WAR ON THE POOR

It's not always easy to put politics aside when examining social issues of this magnitude. When Donald Trump became president, and Jeff Sessions was named attorney general, there was a lot of fear and uncertainty to go around—some of it warranted, some of it not, to be fair.

Sessions was roundly blasted for effectively reinstating a policy that serves as a regressive tax on America's poorest people. The attorney general explained that he sought to do away with "the long-standing abuse of issuing rules by simply publishing a letter or posting a web page." After ordering a reform task force to identify existing guidance documents that go too far, Jeff Sessions revoked more than two dozen such documents going back to 1975 on various topics, including a Reagan-era "industry circular" that stated it was illegal to ship certain guns across a state line. He also issued a recent memo barring the Department of Justice from issuing nonbinding guidances.[19]

After retracting a recent Obama-era guidance to state courts meant to end debtors' prisons, Sessions wrote, "Last month, I ended the longstanding abuse of issuing rules by simply publishing a letter or posting a web page. Congress has provided for a regulatory process in statute, and we are going to follow it. This is good government and prevents confusing the public with improper and wrong advice. Therefore, any guidance that is outdated, used to circumvent the regulatory process, or that improperly goes beyond what is provided for in statutes or regulation should not be given effect. That is why today, we are ending 25 examples of improper or unnecessary guidance documents identified by our Regulatory Reform Task Force led by our Associate Attorney General Rachel Brand. We will continue to look for other examples to rescind, and we will uphold the rule of law."[20]

In response to the criticism, Sessions said that Congress provided for a regulatory process in statute and that they were going to follow it. This move got little notice in the mainstream press or by the public at first, but it has since become a quite a debate. Lisa Foster, who served as director of the Office for Access to Justice at the DOJ, criticized Sessions's move, chastising the Department of Justice for not caring about the United States Constitution in the courts. However, her coauthor, Vanita Gupta, believed that Sessions was already too late to cause too much damage. She thought that the retraction of this guidance didn't change the existing legal framework and that while he can retract the guidance, he can't change what the law said.[21]

Gupta's thought was proven accurate when, just weeks later, a federal court ruled that New Orleans judges faced a conflict of interest in jailing poor people for unpaid fines because the judges control the money collected and rely on it for court funding. And in Michigan, a federal court issued a preliminary injunction halting the state's system for suspending driver's licenses upon nonpayment of traffic tickets due to constitutional concerns. Around the same time, the Mississippi Department of Public Safety agreed to reinstate the driver's licenses of all drivers whose licenses were suspended for nonpayment of court fines and fees. In Missouri, where the troubling resurgence of debtors' prisons first gained national attention, more than a dozen plaintiffs won a class action lawsuit filed against thirteen St. Louis suburbs they accused of conspiring to extort money from poor African American residents via traffic tickets in "a deliberate and coordinated scheme." Even in Sessions's home state of Alabama, a Republican state legislator has sponsored legislation that would do away with debtors' prison.[22]

WHAT'S NOT IN YOUR WALLET

Is this country going to return to the ways of the past when it comes to debt, locking away borrowers who could not afford to pay back their loans inside Victorian-era prisons? Certainly not, but exactly will happen is hard to say.

I don't think it's accurate to say that Attorney General Jeff Sessions and President Trump are for jailing people simply because of their socioeconomic status as some would like to convey, but at the same, time we cannot continue to fine people for nuisance crimes and penalize them financially when they clearly cannot afford to pay the exorbitant fees.

Sustained advocacy and raising awareness continue to be the most effective ways to make your voice heard. Lawmakers are our voice in Washington, and you have to stand up to be heard. Reaching out to groups like your local chapter of the ACLU or the Southern Poverty Law Center is one way to get involved. There are also many prison reform advocacy groups that could benefit from another voice. The following is a partial listing of local prison advocacy and family support organizations across the United States:

PA Prison Society (PPS). 215-564-6005 or 1-(800)-227-2307. 245 N. Broad Street, Suite 300. Philadelphia, PA 19107. geninfo@ prisonsociety.org www.prisonsociety.org/.

The mission of the Pennsylvania Prison Society is to advocate for humane prisons and a rational approach to criminal justice. The Official Visitor Act of 1823, granted by the General Assembly, gives selected Prison Society members legislative authority to visit prisons, monitor conditions statewide and provide a voice for those behind bars; 257 volunteers make more than 2,800 visits each year. $5 Prisoner membership. $10 Family of Prisoner.

Decarcerate PA. 267-217-3372. PO Box 40764. Philadelphia, PA 19107. decaceratePA@gmail.com or decaceratePA.pgh@gmail .com http://decaceratepa.info/.

Decarcerate PA is a grassroots campaign working to end mass incarceration in Pennsylvania. We demand that PA stop building prisons, reduce the prison population, and reinvest money in our communities. Decarcerate PA is a coalition of organizations and individuals seeking an end to mass incarceration and the harms it brings our many communities. Decarcerate PA seeks mechanisms to establish and maintain whole, healthy communities and believes that imprisonment exacerbates the problems we face.

American Friends Service Committee-Healing Justice Program. 1501 Cherry St. Philadelphia, PA 19102. 215-241-7000. http://www.afsc.org/goal/healing-justice.

AFSC opposes maximum security prisons and their lockdown procedures as dehumanizing and violating the Divine Spark within those incarcerated. And we work for the abolition of the death penalty. AFSC calls this healing justice. This program acknowledges that the majority of prisoners will return to the outside world and that communities have a responsibility to aid them as they rejoin society. We have worked with released prisoners on reentry into their communities and have encouraged their families to speak out if they know about abuses or poor treatment in prisons.

Human Rights Coalition—Philly (267) 293-9169. 4134 Lancaster Ave. Philadelphia, PA 19104. http://hrcoalition.org/ info@ hrcoalition.org.

The Human Rights Coalition is a group of predominantly prisoners' families, ex-prisoners, and some supporters. Our ultimate goal is to abolish prisons. We aim to empower prisoners' families to be leaders in prison organizing, while at the same time reduce the shame of having a loved one in prison or being formerly incarcerated. Our goal is to make visible to the public the injustice and abuse that are common practice throughout our judicial and prison systems across the country and eventually end those abuses. We also work to encourage the rehabilitation of prisoners.

Human Rights Coalition—FedUp! 5129 Penn Ave. Pittsburgh, PA 15224. hrcfedup@gmail.com. www.prisonerstories.blogspot.com. 412-361-3022 ext. 4.

Works for the Human Rights of people incarcerated through advocacy. Focus is on people in solitary confinement.

Human Rights Coalition—Chester, Brotha Tut. (610) 876-8226 or (215) 390-41144. hrcchester@yahoo.com.

Human Rights Coalition-Chester Community Resource Center and Outreach Project (HRC-Chester) is comprised of prisoners families, former and current prisoners and concerned citizens working together for prison and re-entry reform and better laws. We also work to build community programs which aim to prevent school dropouts and rally support for remedial programs for High-Risk Youth. HRC-Chester is a branch of the Human Rights Coalition and a regional member of the NAACP's Pennsylvania Prison Project and Education Not Incarceration Delaware Valley.

CentrePeace, Inc. (814) 353-9081. 3013 Benner Pike. Bellefonte, PA 16823. contact@centrepeace.org. www.centrepeace.org.

CentrePeace promotes *Restorative Justice* by modeling programs based on healing brokenness rather than on vengeance- centering on peace rather than fear, offering avenues of accountability rather than alienation. We provide ways for offenders to take responsibility for their lives, resolve problems non-violently and treat others with dignity and respect. We've learned that punishing people by locking them away does little to halt the cycle of crime and violence. Instead, we offer a way to be a contributing member of a working community. Centre County inmates learn valuable job, time management, and socialization skills through working at our Used Household and Furniture Outlet Sale. The inmate volunteers are also required to complete the classes "Creative Non-Violent Conflict Resolution" and "Breaking Barriers" in which they learn to appreciate others' points of view, assume responsibility for mistakes and identify and replace destructive patterns of behavior with positive ones. Criminal Justice Advocacy and Support Directory is compiled by CentrePeace every three years; it is published and distributed free of charge by the Pennsylvania Institutional Law Project. This directory provides listings of services for Pennsylvania inmates, victims and their families. Prayer-Mate Program is a spiritual "pen-pal" system in which participants, using only their first names, communicate through a Centre-Peace coordinator with community volunteers.

Mary Mother of Captives. 215-698-2585. P.O. Box 52416. Philadelphia, PA 19115. mmocsprtgp@aol.com. http://www.marymotherofcaptivessupport.org/.

A Support Group for family and friends who have a loved one in prison, on trial or about to be sentenced to prison. MMOC meets in Northeast Philadelphia and surrounding Counties, ministering to the frustrated, forgotten and innocent victims (the inmate's family). MMOC is open to all regardless of race, creed, color or national origin and is free of any dues. ALL INFORMATION IS STRICTLY CONFIDENTIAL. MMOC now has four monthly meetings: one in the Philadelphia area and one each in Bucks, Chester and Delaware Counties. MMOC has a Pen Pal Program for those who would like to visit an inmate by mail. Encouraging inmates to use the time of incarceration both spiritually and educationally, and to help improve his/her writing skills.

National Prison Advocacy Groups

The Sentencing Project. 1705 DeSales Street, NW 8th Floor. Washington, DC 20036. 202-628-0871. staff@sentencingproject .org. www.sentencingproject.org.

The Sentencing Project was founded in 1986 to provide defense lawyers with sentencing advocacy training and to reduce the reliance on incarceration. As a result of The Sentencing Project's research, publications and advocacy, many people know that this country is the world's leader in incarceration, that one in three young black men is under control of the criminal justice system, that five million Americans can't vote because of felony convictions, and that thousands of women and children have lost welfare, education, and housing benefits as the result of convictions for minor drug offenses.

Critical Resistance National. 1904 Franklin Street, Suite 504. Oakland, CA 94612. 510-444-0484. crnational@criticalresistance .org. http://www.criticalresistance.org

Critical Resistance seeks to build an international movement to end the prison industrial complex (PIC) by challenging the belief that caging and controlling people makes us safe. We believe that basic necessities such as food, shelter, and freedom are what really make our communities secure. As such, our work is part of global struggles against inequality and powerlessness. The success of the movement requires that it reflect communities most affected by the PIC. Because we seek to abolish the PIC, we cannot support any work that extends its life or scope.

Critical Resistance New Orleans. 504-304-3784. 930 N. Broad Street. New Orleans, LA 70119. crno@criticalresistance.org.

Critical Resistance New Orleans is on the front lines of the fight to Stop the expansion of the notorious Orleans Parish Prison. Orleans Parish Prison (OPP) is already the largest per capita county jail of any major US city, while resources for housing, education, job training, and healthcare continue to be cut or remain deeply underfunded. In an effort to stop construction and shrink the prison system in the city, CR-NOLA has been working nonstop with allies and community member, trying to build people power in order to shift vital resources away from the PIC and toward building thriving, sustainable, self-determined communities.

Human Rights Watch. 212-290-4700. 350 Fifth Avenue, 34th Floor. New York, NY 10118. hrwpress@hrw.org. http://www.hrw .org/united-states/us-program/prison-and-detention-conditions press desk.

Human Rights Watch is dedicated to protecting the human rights of people around the world. We stand with victims and activists to prevent discrimination, to uphold political freedom, to protect people from inhumane conduct in wartime, and to bring offenders to justice. We investigate and expose human rights violations and hold abusers accountable. We challenge governments and those who hold power to end abusive practices and respect international human rights law. We enlist the public and the international community to support the cause of human rights for all.

Citizens United for Rehabilitation of Errants (PA CURE). 215-820-7001. P.O. Box 8601. Philadelphia, PA 19101. www .curenational.org.

Support to inmates and families via letters, calls, faxes, and emails. Testifying and attending legislative hearings regarding prison issues. Education about prison issues through visits to prisons and via PA CURE newsletter. Meeting with D.O.C., legislations, regarding policies, inmate and family concerns. High cost of inmate phone calls Elimination of PCN-TV from new Texas cable Being a "Principal" in the Lobbyist Coalition, who has hired Ernest D. Preate Jr. to be our lobbyist regarding prison issues—accompanying Ernie when he speaks at prisons. Holding an Annual PA CURE Rally in Harrisburg. Cooperating and networking with and supporting other prison advocacy organizations.

Chicano Mexicano Prison Project/Union del Barrio. P.O. Box 13036. San Diego, CA 92170. 619-398-6648. info@uniondelbarrio .org. http://www.uniondelbarrio.org.

CMPP is committed to continue the struggle for the human rights of prisoners and the liberation of the Mexicano Indigenous people.

Prison Activist Resource Center (PARC). P.O. Box 70447. Oakland, CA 94612. 510-893-4648. info@prisonactivist.org, prisonactivist@gmail.com. www.prisonactivist.org.

PARC is a prison abolitionist group committed to exposing and challenging all forms of institutionalized racism, sexism, able-ism, heterosexism, and classism, specifically within the Prison Industrial Complex (PIC). PARC believes in building strategies and tactics that build safety in our communities without reliance on the police or the PIC. We produce a directory that is free to prisoners upon request and seek to work in solidarity with prisoners, ex-prisoners, their friends, and families.

Amnesty International USA. 5 Penn Plaza. New York, NY 10001. 212-807-8400. aimember@aiusa.org.

Amnesty Mid-Atlantic Regional Office. 600 Penn. Ave., SE5th Floor. Washington, DC 20003. 202-544-0200. aiusama@aiusa.org. www.amnestyusa.org.

Families Against Mandatory Minimums (FAMM). National Office: 1100 H Street NW Suite 1000. Washington, DC 20005. 202-822-6700. famm@famm.org. www.famm.org.

FAMM (Families Against Mandatory Minimums) is a nonprofit, nonpartisan organization fighting for fair and proportionate sentencing laws that allow judicial discretion while maintaining public safety.

Just Detention International (formerly Stop Prisoner Rape). 3325 Wilshire Blvd, Suite 340. Los Angeles, CA 90010. 213-384-1400. info@justdetention.org.

Just Detention International is a health and human rights organization that seeks to end sexual abuse in all forms of detention. If you are incarcerated, please feel free to communicate with JDI using legal mail, addressing your correspondence to: Cynthia Totten, Esq. CA Attorney Reg. #199266 3325 Wilshire Blvd., Suite 340. LA, CA 90010.

American-Arab Anti Discrimination Committee. 1990 M Street, NW, Suite 610. Washington, DC 20036. 202-244-2990. www.adc.org.

Provides advice, referrals, full-time staff attorneys to help defend interest of the community; also serves as a vital clearinghouse of accurate information on Arab culture and history for education and school systems.

The November Coalition Foundation. 282 West Astor Ave. Colville, WA 99114. 509-684-1550. moreinfo@november.org. http://www.november.org.

Focus on the drug war, great resource on the web, also have a newsletter.[23]

12

FEDERAL PRISON— MY PERSONAL JOURNEY

I GREW UP with a father who did not want to be a part of my life. He left my mother when I was six months old to be with another woman, whom he later married and with whom he had had two sons, half-brothers whom I never knew.

It was a struggle for my mother to raise me alone, and as I grew, so did my resentment toward my father, so much so that when my mom remarried, I asked my stepfather to adopt me so I could take his name. Suddenly, not only did I have a new last name, but I had a dad who did all the things with me that other kids' dads did with them. I was part of a big Italian family that were together all the time and yelled at one another when they talked. It took me a little while to realize that they weren't mad at one another. They truly loved one another and loved being together.

All along, my paternal grandparents did all they could on my behalf, overcompensating when it came to my future. Both history buffs, they took me on trips to many of the historic sites around the region and country, stimulating my early interest in government. From a young age, they always told me that I would be a lawyer one day. Their constant support and the confidence they instilled in me had a huge impact.

Getting involved in politics was not something that was even on my radar until I decided to run for Student Council in high school. My neighborhood friend, Stephen Ucci, was older and on the Student Council, so I decided to run. Besides Stephen, who is a current Rhode Island State representative, Gina Raimundo, our present state governor, was also on the school Student Council with me in high school. This was when I discovered that I had a genuine interest in public service.

It was a simple start, and I began getting more involved and counted on to get things done. I certainly didn't know much about real politics then, but I learned that people got into politics for different reasons, and not all of them good ones. I can honestly say that I didn't go for any of that. I truly wanted to help people.

I took up political science at Providence College and later got an internship in the office of the charismatic Providence mayor, Vincent "Buddy" Cianci. During college, I also worked on many local campaigns, including those of the City Council in Providence, state representative, and senator, as well as campaigns for governor and state treasurer.

One of the first things that happened to me when I became a senator was to receive an early morning call from an older woman who told me she had no heat in her home. She and her husband had a boiler installed by Tri-Town Community Action Agency, which helped low-income people with heating assistance. I wondered why she was calling me and how she got my number, but I thought this is why I got into politics, so I told the couple to give me a few minutes, and I would call them back. I tried calling the agency, but of course, no one was there, so I contacted a friend who was in the heating and air conditioning business. I offered to pay him out of my pocket if he would go over to the couple's house and see if he could remedy their heating problem. My friend quickly determined that the contractor who installed the system wired the thermostat incorrectly. It took fifteen minutes to fix the problem, and it was a nice moment because I had been able to help these people.

My initiation into the Rhode Island political arena was in September 2006, when I won the primary election. The Senate Democratic Leadership reached out to bring me into the fold, and I quickly learned what it was all about. I didn't have a general election, because my town consisted predominantly of Democrats. In fact, since the Great Depression, Democrats have been the majority party in Rhode Island. Johnston is full of people who work for unions, including teachers, firemen, police, state employees, laborers, and prison guards. To have the endorsement of the teachers or firefighters, in particular, meant a lot. I got the endorsement of both. It didn't hurt that my wife was a public school teacher and my father a retired fireman. The town has the second largest Italian population in the nation, which means a large contingency of Catholic voters. Being pro-life was helpful to get the backing of the Church. The other big "one-issue group" in Johnston is the NRA. You could propose to build a nuclear power plant in their backyard, but as long as you were pro-gun and pro-life, you were guaranteed their votes, which I got; this was called having the "backing of God and Guns." The NRA was good at informing their supporters who supported their issues. I remember going to people's houses and seeing signs that said, "If you're not pro-gun, don't bother knocking."

Then there were the lies and the rumors that legislators would spread about one another to try to influence me to one side or another. Not to mention the anonymous accusations made against me, including generating rumors of infidelity, a tactic that was very common because of the intense rivalry and jealousy among politicians, even the ones in your own party. These are things young senators are not told about before entering politics in Rhode Island. There were a lot more lessons to follow as I got to know the other legislators and the mayor, which turned out to be vastly different from what I experienced while working in the office of Providence mayor Buddy Cianci.

OPERATION DOLLAR BILL

"Operation Dollar Bill" was an undercover investigation by the FBI into corruption within the state of Rhode Island that stemmed from allegations that first emerged in 2003 regarding State Senator John Celona, who had accepted money and gifts from CVS, Blue Cross & Blue Shield of Rhode Island, and Roger Williams Hospital. Charges were filed against Celona in 2005 by a United States attorney claiming that the senator defrauded the state's citizens by accepting money and gifts from those companies, which had interests in legislation Celona considered as chairman of the Senate Corporations Committee. Celona had agreed to cooperate with investigators before the charges were filed against him.

Even with Celona's cooperation, the investigation, which involved the FBI, Rhode Island State Police, the Internal Revenue Service, and the United States Department of Labor, turned out to be a total failure. Operation Dollar Bill was widely criticized by many people, including former mayor Vincent "Buddy" Cianci, who facetiously referred to it as "Operation Fifty Cent." The only conviction brought by the probe was to Gerard M. Martineau, the Rhode Island House majority leader, who pleaded guilty in November 2007 to honest services mail fraud for engaging in extensive and undisclosed personal business dealings. Celona's bribes were provided by the chairman of Roger Williams Medical Center, Robert Urciuoli, who was convicted of conspiracy and dozens of counts of mail fraud.

Other politicians investigated included the state's senate president, Joseph Montalbano, and Senate Finance Committee Chairman Stephen Alves, as well as the Senate's deputy majority whip, Daniel DaPonte. A pair of Democrat state representatives, John DeSimone and Robert Flaherty, were also named in the probe for their relationship to an insurance company.

The convictions of two former Roger Williams Medical Center executives were later vacated by a federal appeals court. Robert A. Urciuoli, the former Roger Williams' president and CEO, had been convicted of charges related to stealing the honest services of former state senator John A. Celona by paying him for political favors; and Frances P. Driscoll, the medical center's former vice president, had been found guilty of one count of mail fraud.

The failure of this investigation left the feds desperate for corruption convictions in the state, and as a result, they were ready to play hardball with anybody they had something on and could use for their purposes.

THE START OF A NEW INVESTIGATION

Toward the end of the session in June 2007, the Johnston mayor announced that a trucking company, A. Duie Pyle, was planning to build a distribution facility in the town. The business was seeking "project status" from the General Assembly, which normally goes through the State Economic Development Corporation before a bill is passed to confirm the status. With the session drawing to an end for the year, the company asked for the resolution to be introduced and passed to avoid any delays. Such requests are not unusual and are granted all the time. This one was a no-brainer: a project that was good for the state, as well as the town, both of whom were in desperate need of new jobs and tax revenue. I had the bill prepared, but because we were in the final few weeks of the session, permission of the Senate leadership was required. I took it to the majority whip, who soon came back to me and told me that Senator Stephen Alves "doesn't like the bill," so I did not put it in.

The mayor was not happy about this, and the belief was that Alves killed the bill simply because the mayor did not give the town's pension business to Alves. This was my first legislative session, so I had no say in the matter, at least until a few months later, when I got a call from an investigative reporter who wanted to talk to me about the matter, which I did. On September 30, an article about the bill and delay was printed in the *Providence Journal*, causing a big stir in the state's political talk show circuit. Around that time, the FBI contacted me, making it clear that Senator Alves was under investigation and that the mayor was speaking to the Feds, something I had refused to do until I received a subpoena from the FBI to testify before a federal Grand Jury. Even for an attorney, an appearance before a Grand Jury can be intimidating, which in my opinion was the FBI's intent. In this process, there is no judge or attorney present, which makes everyone involved appear (and feel) guilty of something, even if they are not. One of the prosecutors who questioned me is now a state Superior Court judge.

I was in the Grand Jury room for about an hour, and the answers I provided were exactly the same answers I had told the journalist previously, and it was nothing that would rise to the level of criminality on the part of Steve Alves. Maybe what he did could be considered wrong, dirty, or possibly even revengeful, but it was not illegal.

After my appearance, it was obvious to me that the Feds purposely leaked information to the members of the media. Why that is, I do not know, but it sure was smart on their part; now the politician (me) has a fight on two fronts. The legal front, and now the public relations front, because the news of an investigation is not something any politician wants to see go public, whether you did anything wrong or not; it's always damaging. For me, the trickle-down effect of this would change my life in profound ways that I had not anticipated.

Early one morning, I answered a knock on my door as I was getting my school-age children ready for the day and was greeted by the stern expressions of a strange man and woman. With their FBI badges displayed, I was told that they were here to arrest me. With my six-year-old daughter asking me questions that were difficult to answer, such as "Why are you being arrested, Dad?" I was permitted to take my kids to school with the caveat that I return home immediately afterward. I noticed right away that I was being followed by two agents who didn't make any effort to hide it. Although the Feds advised me not to tell anyone about their sudden appearance, I felt compelled to call a friend and lawyer, as well as another attorney, who practiced federal criminal law in Boston. I returned home to find a dozen cars in my driveway, and while the agents were not happy when my attorney-friend arrived, they finally revealed the hand they wanted to play when they showed me a copy of my tax return and asked about the mortgage on my house. After I told him that I paid off the loan earlier that year, one of the agents said he didn't care about mortgages, informing me that they were from the public corruption unit and they wanted me to help them. I got on the phone with Bill Kettlewell, my defense attorney, and had him speak with the female agent. After she hung up, she got up and announced they were leaving, cautioning me again not to speak to anyone about their visit to my house.

"Do you have a warrant?" I asked as they were leaving.

One of them then produced an arrest warrant, and I could plainly see that it was blank.

I would come to understand then that the Feds were not really interested in me, but they would take me if I could not help them make corruption cases against my friends. The Feds showed early on that they were ready to play hardball with me, prepared to take it all the way, even pull me away from my family and take both of our children away from their mother by threatening to prosecute my wife because her name was also on the bank documents.

MY FRIENDS ARE NOT FOR SALE

My own government proceeded to build a case against me on multiple charges of bank fraud and at the same time tried to pressure me into working with them. While I was under investigation, one of the first things my lawyer told me was that if this case had come across his desk, he would never have pursued it. He had a lot of experience, previously serving as an assistant US attorney, and he was chief of the President's Organized Crime and Drug Task Force for New England and later became chief of the Criminal Division for the District of Massachusetts.

When my lawyer met with the assistant US attorney, it became crystal clear that it did not matter to the Feds that the majority of my loans had been paid in full, with the properties either sold or refinanced, while the remaining loans were current and being paid on time, and not in default. However, it was also revealed that the Feds were capable of making all my problems go away if I helped them build a public corruption case against other politicians in the state, or even at the municipal level in the town of Johnston.

Clearly, they did not want me, and I made it clear to them I had no intention of helping the FBI. I told them that I didn't know anything and that even if anyone were doing something wrong, I didn't see it, didn't hear about it, and no one spoke about it. It was sort of like the three monkeys: hear no evil, see no evil, and speak no evil. As I was a new legislator, did the FBI really think that anyone would have confided in me, opening up about all the bad things they did?

When I asked my attorney why the Feds came to me, he told me that I fit the profile of what they were looking for—a young guy with a family, successful, and up-and-coming in politics—and they didn't think I would be willing to jeopardize that. My attorney didn't think I was the only one they approached, and maybe one of the others would cooperate, so he advised me to keep quiet about it and bide my time. He would always say that "time was my friend," assuring me that the more time that passed, the better it would be for me. So that's what we did, but the Feds kept calling my attorney, and finally, he told them that I had nothing for them.

"Maybe he doesn't," the Feds responded, "but he has a lot of friends at the statehouse and other places in government. He can still help us. He can wear a wire and set up meetings for us."

"*No way!*" was my response to their fishing expedition. That's not me. I went to lunch or dinner with very few people from the statehouse, and the ones I did go with are my close friends.

I wanted to go public and hold a press conference on the stairs of the statehouse to let the world know that the FBI was trying to squeeze me. However, my lawyer cautioned me that such a plan would surely backfire on me and that my best bet was to keep my mouth shut, just the opposite of what the Feds wanted me to do.

MY INDICTMENT

On Memorial Day weekend 2010, I ran out of time with the Feds. They wanted something I was never going to give them, and that's when they closed the noose around my neck. I was indicted on seven counts of bank fraud, and in order to keep my wife out of trouble, an additional count of bank fraud, alleging that I used a family member as a straw borrower and fabricated documents to support the loan application, was added.

According to investigators from the FBI, along with US Department of Housing & Urban Development (HUD), the Office of the Inspector General, and the Internal Revenue Service, Criminal Investigations, between June 2007 and March 2009, I had applied for and received several bank loans, primarily mortgage loans, and that in order to qualify for those loans, I lied about my income and assets, producing fabricated documentation, including false tax returns and bank statements. They alleged that I had my wife sign a purchase and sale agreement to buy land and a home for $200,000 with the intention of demolishing the existing structure to build a new house. They claimed I used my wife's elderly grandmother as a straw borrower, as well, applying for two mortgages in her name, totaling $200,000. To pull off this fraud, they claimed I created false documents and submitted false information on the loan applications, and then after the closing, they said I completed a deed transfer that transferred her ownership in the property to me.

The reality was far less nefarious than how the Feds wanted to portray it. All of the property in question was bought for my personal use and used by my family. I was not flipping houses for profit. I bought my first house, a two-family home, and refinanced it to get a better rate. As my family grew, I purchased a single family home and kept the two-family to rent. I refinanced the single-family home to get a better rate. When the single-family home became too small for my family, I sold it, paid off the mortgage, and purchased a bigger single-family home. I refinanced that to get a better rate. At no time did I ever take cash out at a refinance. Many times, I brought money to the closing table to pay for closing costs so they didn't get rolled into the loan.

My real problem was educational debt and being self-employed. My debt-to-income ratio was high. Both my wife and I had loans from college and law school. My school loans alone totaled over $100,000, so I fell into the trap, like so many others: I inflated my income to make my debt-to-income ratio fit the qualifications to get the loan. The trap that had been set up by the major banks, inadvertent or not, was that they were giving away money in stated income deals, so banks did not verify income. The real winner in all this was the banks that were selling these mortgages and making millions. In the end, we, the American taxpayers, bailed all the banks out because they were too big to fail.

OPERATION "STOLEN DREAMS"

Of course, this banking crisis cost taxpayers $700 billion when Congress passed a bank bailout bill in October 2008 to buy mortgage-backed securities that were in danger of defaulting, thereby taking these debts off the books of the banks, hedge funds, and pension funds that held them.

In March 2010, Operation Stolen Dreams was launched, which became the largest collective enforcement effort brought to bear in confronting mortgage fraud. The federal sweep was established to lead an aggressive, coordinated, and proactive effort to investigate and prosecute financial crimes. FBI agents and analysts worked together using intelligence, enhanced surveillance, and undercover operations to identify emerging trends and to find the key players behind large-scale fraud.

Within three months, Operation Stolen Dreams involved 1,215 criminal defendants nationwide, including 485 arrests, which were allegedly responsible for more than $2.3 billion in losses. Unlike previous mortgage fraud sweeps, Operation Stolen Dreams focused not only on federal criminal cases, but also on civil enforcement and restitution for victims. Federal agencies participating included the Department of Housing and Urban Development, the Treasury Department, the Federal Trade Commission, the Internal Revenue Service, the US Postal Inspection Service, and the US Secret Service. Many state and local agencies were also involved in the operation.

A wide net was cast, in which I got caught, even though I was just bait fish for what the Feds really wanted in their hooks.

For me, as an attorney, I was handling several closing transactions per week at that time. I saw it all, from the mortgage brokers making hundreds of thousands of dollars off transactions, to people who were refinancing their homes two and three times a year to cash out their equity in their house, using their house as a personal ATM. The banks were just throwing money at people. I called it "Dialing-For-Dollars." Mortgage brokers had telemarketers cold-calling people all day long and closing deals that sometimes yielded in excess of $10,000 on a single transaction. They would charge fees to the client, and then the banks would give them their point spread on the back end (a commission for getting the loan). They were putting people in interest-only loans, loans with one- and five-year balloon payments; bad deals all the way around. I saw thousands of transactions where there was no way these people could afford these loans, but they got them anyway.

THE PLEA AND HYPOCRISY ON THE BENCH

During the entire year when this indictment had been hanging over my head, I believed that the Feds were just shaking me down, trying to scare me into helping them. From the first day they showed up on my doorstep with a blank arrest warrant, they told me directly that it was not about mortgages; it was about public corruption, and they wanted me to help them. Fast-forward a little: when push came to shove, they indicted me under Operation Stolen Dream. That was June 17, 2010, and it was the very same day that every state in the country indicted people on mortgage fraud or related charges. The operation was obviously a directive straight from Washington, a symbolic public display to show that they were confronting and dealing with this problem. In most states, numerous defendants were charged on this federal mandate, but in Rhode Island, I was the only person named and indicted. That year, according to the annual Mortgage Fraud Investigation Report, Rhode Island was fifth in the nation for mortgage fraud investigations, yet I was the only one indicted.

Hypocrisy was rife when it came to my indictment, and so was it present when it came time to "cop a plea,": I changing my plea from *not guilty* to *guilty* on federal bank fraud charges. I didn't know at that time what sentence I would be receiving, even though all the papers were reporting that bank fraud was an offense punishable by a maximum sentence of thirty years' imprisonment, a $1 million fine, and five years of supervised release. While fully aware that jail time was a possibility, I was optimistic about avoiding prison as a prime candidate for home confinement so that I could continue working, paying my bills, and supporting my family.

Man plans and God laughs, or so it goes.

What happened in court that day was that in exchange for my admission of guilt, the US Attorney offered me a flat twenty-four-month prison sentence. Upon hearing the length of the sentence, I was completely stunned. I expressed my concerns to my attorney, who assured me that mine was a home confinement case all day long and that even if they wanted to make an example out of me, no judge would give me anything more than a year, at most, and I believed him. I didn't feel there was any reason not to take him at his word. I asked him directly what my options were, and he told me that I could either accept the plea agreement they offered, knowing up front that it would be a twenty-four-month prison stint. Or I could enter what was called an *open plea*, which is when both sides make their arguments to a judge, who would decide how much time I should get. With the second option, I would be putting my fate in the hands of the judge. It would be a gamble, but there was a really good chance that a judge would realize that serving any kind of time was not warranted in my case. What also gave me hope was knowing that some of those defendants had actually stolen money and were given no jail time by the same judge. Furthermore, I believed that the latitude granted the judge in the application of federal sentencing guidelines would work in my favor. A big fine, with home confinement and probation, was what I thought I would be getting.

What I didn't realize was that the presiding judge never practiced a single day of law in her life. She was a political appointee from the start. Her father petitioned to get her a job with the state right out of law school. Before ascending to the bench, she worked in the Child's Advocate Office and then served as the Disciplinary Counsel for Rhode Island, a post where her job was metering out punishment to lawyers who did wrong.

Still, you expect that the judge would be fair and impartial, leaving it up to the prosecutor to build a strong case against a defendant to get the sentence they are seeking. My judge, however, went so far as to pull my case from another judge to whom it had originally been assigned. So I had unwittingly put my fate in the hands of a judge who seemed to have a predilection for taking cases involving lawyers and politicians accused of an offense and disciplining them to the fullest extent of the law.

Apparently, the judge's heart was set on making an example out of me, and the court imposed a twenty-seven-month sentence on me, three months more than what the Feds offere: a sort of penalty for not playing ball.

So why would I even take an open plea deal to begin with, some people might ask, especially when prison time remained a distinct possibility?

My lawyer did not push me to take a deal. He told me from the start that he thought he had a better than fair chance of winning the case in court.

Only a few clients of all the ones he represented in Federal Court had he recommended going to a jury trial, and mine was one of them. In the court-room, my lawyer would reason that no one had been hurt by what I did and that the banks weren't complaining. In fact, with the right jury, the banks could be put on trial. They were the ones who profited. He was prepared to argue that the bank never bothered to confirm that the income information provided by loan applicants is correct, which the institution had a right to do, as allowed by a special IRS tax form in the mortgage application. The fact is that banks not only wanted the loan, they wanted the interest. Ini-tially, I was very excited about my chances, and I wanted to go down the path of letting a jury of my peers decide my fate from all the evidence and testimony given by both sides. It wasn't long after I informed the FBI through my attorney that we would not be open to a plea deal and that we were lean-ing toward trying the case in court that my wife received a call on her cell phone from the Feds telling her that she was going to be charged with mort-gage fraud. They also sent her a "target letter," informing her that she was under investigation and suggested that she come in to federal court and plead guilty. These strong-arm tactics worked because she immediately began to panic. She was forced to get a lawyer, and even though there was no real substance to the letter, and the whole thing was obviously a threat to influence me to drop any idea I had of taking my case to trial, my hands were effectively tied. My wife was a school teacher, and she was not only afraid of the ramifications this kind of public embarrassment would have on her, but also of how it would affect our son and daughter. I had no choice but to drop the jury trial and look into the next best option. I opted for the open plea because in return for leaving my wife out of this mess, the Feds were asking me to take a deal that included the possibility of twenty-four months in prison. Still, my lawyer still did not feel this was a jail case, and neither did I. So I opted for the open plea.

At this point, there was nothing I could do. By being sentenced to prison, I could no longer work and would not be able to pay the bank off on the remaining loans I had. The bank lost money, I lost my freedom, and the judge did not sympathize with either of us, wanting to make it absolutely clear to me that my mistake was the reason everything happened the way it did.

Admittedly, I broke the law. I cannot deny or defend my actions. I was wrong and fully expected to be disciplined for knowingly giving false information on federal banking documents, and now I accepted that I was going to prison for twenty-seven months. I had exactly one month to report to Fort Dix Federal Prison in New Jersey.

Those thirty days were a blur of apprehension and uncertainty. Each succeeding day went by faster than the one before.

Then, my time was up. In the final twenty-four hours before reporting to federal prison, the hardest thing I ever had to do was saying good-bye to my children, which I tried to make as easy as possible, telling them I would be home soon. The following day, my wife, along with my best friend and his wife drove me to Fort Dix Federal Prison in New Jersey. We left the day before I was scheduled to turn myself in, stopping over in New York City. The plan was to break the drive up and spend the night in the City: a little send-off before I surrendered to federal authorities.

The stress of the incident fractured my damaged marriage permanently. Our relationship had begun to unravel quickly soon after I was charged, and it became clear to both of us by the time we left for New York that our relationship would not survive. I knew then that when it was all over, and I was released from prison, I would no longer be married. I would, in fact, receive divorce papers while I was in prison.

PRISON LIFE

The reality of being confined in a cell was something I had to come to terms with, and I had to quickly adapt to the daily routine and discipline that is so much a part of prison life. I had a job in prison, I could have visitors and read a lot of books, and considering the kind of time I was doing and where I was, it could have been a lot worse. It was not the hard time most people think of from the popular books and movies. But it wasn't like Ray Liotta in *Goodfellas*, either.

I did my time with some interesting inmates, unique characters and diverse personalities that exposed me to a whole different side of life. The experiences and personal interactions I had with these individuals changed my outlook on life and how I looked at myself.

Before I surrendered to Fort Dix, I had friends reach out to anyone they might know at the federal prison. It turned out someone I knew had a family member at Fort Dix, and it was Matthew "Matty" Guglielmetti, a reputed capo in the New England Mafia and close associate of former mob boss Raymond "Junior" Patriarca. They let Matty know I was coming, so when I arrived in the camp building, word got back to him that I was there. I had been there less than an hour when Matty approached me. I was sitting on my bunk talking with the other guys, who were asking questions, like where I was from and what I did for work. They were trying to feel me out to see if I was "good," or if I was a "rat." New guys were sometimes asked to show them their papers, meaning sentencing papers. If you cooperated with the government, it would show a reduction in sentencing guidelines under 5K1.1. Guys in prison called it a 5K1.

I was having a conversation with my bunkmate, who was called "Panama," and another guy called "O," when everyone stopped and turned to look at Matty as he approached and stopped near the foot of my bunk. He was holding a bag and said hello to me like he had known me his whole life. I got up to greet him, and he handed me a "welcome" bag, which contained a toothbrush, toothpaste, shower shoes, and a pair of sweats, stuff a new inmate needs to get through the next day until he could get to the commissary. Panama and O both turned to Matty, and one of them asked, "You know him?"

Matty said, "Yes."

"So, he is good?" Matty was asked.

"Yeah, he's good."

And with that, all the tension, which just moments before was thick enough to cut with a knife, just disappeared.

Matty then said to me, "Come on. Let's get something to eat." And off I went to the cafeteria to have my first prison meal: meatloaf.

RELEASE FROM PRISON

During the last six weeks of my sentence, I was released into a halfway house, a place that helps many inmates reintegrate back into society before they are released. Coolidge House is a local facility in Brookline, Massachusetts, where most federal inmates finishing up their time at Fort Dix are sent. While preparing inmates for the outside world, facilities like Coolidge House afford the men many privileges. Not only are you not confined, but you can also leave the facility, get on a train or bus, travel to Rhode Island or anywhere else, just as long as you're back before a certain time: there is a curfew. You could go to the YMCA nearby, order pizza, and go to work during the day. You're in a room with a bunch of guys sleeping in bunks like you see in the army, but you can come and go pretty much as you please.

For some reason, however, I didn't get sent to Coolidge House. Instead, I went to the Barnstable County Correction Facility in Bourne, Massachusetts, which in many ways was worse than the federal prison I had just left. I was locked in a cell twenty-two hours a day, only getting out when I went on work release. I was unable to move around or go outside. I couldn't exercise or watch TV.

I'm not mentioning this because I want anyone to feel sorry for me, but just as a way of comparing Fort Dix with Barnstable County Correction. What was supposed to be a transitional period for me was even more restrictive. I went from minimum security to max. There were a couple of other guys with me in Barnstable who had come from other federal prisons, all from higher security facilities than I.

Finally, that six-week stretch ended, and I was free, but I knew that I could not just pick up where I had left things before I went in. There were a lot of little adjustments. It was hard for me to sleep, having gotten used to people walking by me all the time with flashlights shining in my face. The food was very bland in prison, and my stomach needed to get used to what I was eating at home. I was a good twenty pounds lighter. There were some big changes, as well. My license to practice law was gone for five years, my marriage was completely over, and the house was gone, but what I wanted more than anything else was to reconnect with my kids. Trying to make up for lost time was the hardest thing for me. They had changed, and so had I, and I knew it would take a while. My son and daughter suffered through that time every bit as much as I did, more, in fact: having their family ripped apart, moving and changing schools, and losing all their friends.

I worked at a friend's father's auto body shop, and I slowly began putting the pieces back together.

THE NEED FOR PRISON REFORM

I feel very strongly about prison reform. Before being sent to prison, I knew that there were inherent deficiencies with our criminal justice system with regard to how certain crimes resulted in certain segments of the population being disproportionately incarcerated. However, I was not aware that there was such a serious need for reform when it came to how sentence length needs to be changed in order to better accommodate the many inmates in prison facilities around the country. The United States makes up a small percentage of the world population (less than 5 percent), yet our incarcerated inmates account for one-quarter of all inmates in the world.

· I feel that the rate of recidivism is never going to change until inmates are given a real chance to succeed, in the form of education and job training, which are two things many people released from prison do not have. You have to give them more than what they have, and a serious commitment must be made to invest in them. I believe there would be a substantive return on the investment, because if you give them the proper tools they need for success, whether it is teaching them a trade, providing them with an education, or just changing the expungement laws, they will have choices other than returning to crime. Federal crimes cannot be expunged, and that follows a person applying for a job, so just changing the laws so that after they do their time, they are forgiven when they get out. This will give them a fair chance and the ability to break the cycle of reoffending and reincarceration. I was lucky; I had an education and a second chance to get my license back, so that I could go back into practice. Most people don't have such opportunities, and it ends up affecting all of us. Taxpayers foot the bill for everyone in our prison system, and I believe a lot of that money would be better spent on education and job services.

Chapter 1

1. E2BN "Victorian Crime and Punishment." *19th Century Justice*. 2006. Accessed January 21, 2018. http://vcp.e2bn.org/.
2. E2BN "Victorian Crime and Punishment." *Transportation*. 2006. Accessed January 21, 2018. http://vcp.e2bn.org/justice/section2196-transportation .html.
3. E2BN "Victorian Crime and Punishment." *Sentences and Punishments*. 2006. Accessed January 21, 2018. http://vcp.e2bn.org/justice/page11361-types-of -punishment-imprisonment.html.
4. Ibid.
5. Ramsey, David. "The Ballad of Reading Gaol—History of the Poem." *Gradesaver*. 1999. Accessed January 21, 2018. http://www.gradesaver.com /the-ballad-of-reading-gaol/wikipedia/history-of-the-poem.
6. Wilde, Oscar. "The Ballard of Reading Gaol." 1896. Accessed January 22, 2018. http://www.gutenberg.org/files/301/301-h/301-h.htm.
7. E2BN "Victorian Crime and Punishment." *Sentences and Punishments*. 2006. Accessed January 21, 2018. http://vcp.e2bn.org/justice/page11361-types-of -punishment-imprisonment.html.
8. Joshi, Vaijayanti. "Victorian Era England Debtors' Prisons History & Living Conditions." Victorian-Era.org. Accessed January 22, 2018. http://www .victorian-era.org/debt-prisons-of-victorian-era-england.html.
9. Ware, Stephen J. "A 20th Century Debate About Imprisonment for Debt." *American Journal of Legal History*. July 2014.

10. Johnson, Paul. "Creditors, Debtors and the Law in Victorian and Edwardian England." May 1996.

11. Skipper, James. "Wages and Cost of Living in the Victorian Era. The Victorian Web. July 16, 2003. Accessed January 22, 2018. http://www .victorianweb.org/economics/wages2.html.

12. Joshi, Vaijayanti. "Victorian Era Prisons." Victorian-Era.org. Accessed January 22, 2018. http://www.victorian-era.org/victorian-era-prisons.html.

13. Wilkes, Jonny. "In a Nutshell: Debtors' Prisons Revealed." *History Revealed*. February 10, 2015. Accessed January 22, 2018. http://www.historyrevealed .com/facts/nutshell-debtors'-prisons.

14. Baxley, James. "What was a Victorian Debt Prison?" Quora. March 13, 2016. Accessed January 22, 2018. https://www.quora.com/What-was-a-Victorian -debt-prison.

15. Marshalsea: Wikis. Accessed January 22, 2018..http://www.thefullwiki.org /Marshalsea.

16. Ibid.

17. Ibid.

18. Jot101. "A Begging Letter from a Debtors' Prison." *Jot101*. August 19, 2015. Accessed January 22, 2018. http://jot101ok.blogspot.com/2015/08/a-begging -letter-from-debtors-prison.html.

19. Everipedia. "Marshalsea." Accessed January 22, 2018. https://everipedia.org /wiki/Marshalsea/.

20. Shmoop Editorial Team. "Newgate Prison in Moll Flanders." Shmoop University, Inc. Last modified November 11, 2008. Accessed January 22, 2018. https://www.shmoop.com/moll-flanders/newgate-prison-symbol.html.

21. Dickens, Charles. "Visit to Newgate—by Charles Dickens's Sketches by Boz." British Library. Accessed January 22, 2018. https://www.bl.uk/collection -items/a-visit-to-newgate-from-charles-dickenss-sketches-by-boz.

22. "History of the United Kingdom." Wikipedia. Accessed January 22, 2018. https://en.wikipedia.org/wiki/History_of_the_United_Kingdom.

23. Rosen, Bruce. "Income and Expenditure in Working-Class Victorian England." *Victorian History*. June 19, 2014. Accessed January 22, 2018. http:// vichist.blogspot.com/2014/.

24. McDaniel, Bethany. "Georgia Found 281 Years Ago Today." *Georgia.gov.* February 12, 2014. Accessed January 22, 2018. https://georgia.gov/blog/2014 -02-12/georgia-founded-281-years-ago-today.

25. Baxley, James. "What was a Victorian Debt Prison?" Quora. March 13, 2016. Accessed January 22, 2018. https://www.quora.com/What-was-a-Victorian -debt-prison.

26. Everipedia. Debtors' Act of 1869. Accessed January 22, 2018. https:// everipedia.org/wiki/Debtors_Act_1869/.

27. Ibid.

28. Hawthorne, Nathaniel. *The Scarlet Letter.* Accessed January 22, 2018.

29. https://www.cliffsnotes.com/literature/s/the-scarlet-letter/summary-and -analysis/chapter-1/chapter-1-1.

30. USHistory.org. Pre-Columbian to the New Millennium. Accessed January 22, 2018. http://www.ushistory.org/us/2c.asp.

31. Bowers, Devon. "The Shackles Return: Why Debtors' Prisons are Making an American Comeback." Activist Post. February 27, 2015. Accessed January 22, 2018. https://www.prisonlegalnews.org/news/2015/feb/27/shackles-return -why-debtors-prisons-are-making-american-comeback/.

32. Ibid.

33. Wood, Betty. "Slavery in Colonial Georgia." New Georgia Encyclopedia. September 24, 2014. Accessed January 23, 2018. https://www .georgiaencyclopedia.org/articles/history-archaeology/slavery-colonial-georgia.

34. Historic Northampton & Museum Center. "Shay's Rebellion." Accessed January 24, 2018. http://www.historic-northampton.org/highlights/shays.html.

35. American Revolutionary War History. Revwartalk.com. Accessed January 24, 2018. https://www.revwartalk.com/Continental-Congressmen-Pennsylvania /robert-morris.html.

36. Fraser, Steve. "The Politics of Debt in America." The History News Network. January 29, 2013. Accessed January 24, 2018. http://historynewsnetwork.org /article/150392.

37. New World Encyclopedia. "Bankruptcy." Accessed January 24, 2018. http:// web.newworldencyclopedia.org/entry/Bankruptcy.

Chapter 2

1. Mount, Steve. "Amendment 14—Citizenship Rights." USConstitution.net. November 30, 2011. Accessed January 20, 2018. https://www.usconstitution .net/xconst_Am14.html

2. Kelly, Martin. "14th Amendment Summary." ThoughtCo. July 27, 2017. Accessed January 20, 2018. https://www.thoughtco.com/us-constitution-14th -amendment-summary-105382

3. Canfield, Sabrina. "Judge Finds New Orleans Debtors' Prison Unconstitutional." Courthouse News. December 15, 2017. Accessed January 20, 2018. https://www.courthousenews.com/judge-finds-new-orleans-debtors-prison -unconstitutional/

4. Ibid.

5. Gibson, Kate. "How You Could Go to Debtors' Prison in the US" MoneyWatch. March 21. 2016. Accessed January 21, 2018. https://www.cbsnews .com/news/how-you-could-go-to-debtors-prison-in-the-u-s/.

6. Choudhury, Nusrat. "Jeff Sessions Takes a Stand on Debtors' Prisons." ACLU. December 28, 2017. Accessed January 20, 2018. https://www.aclu.org/blog /racial-justice/race-and-criminal-justice/jeff-sessions-takes-stand-debtors -prisons.

7. Pishko, Jessica. "Locked up for Being Poor." February 25, 2015. *The Atlantic*. Accessed January 20, 2018. https://www.theatlantic.com/national/archive /2015/02/locked-up-for-being-poor/386069/.

8. Bearden vs. Georgia, 461 U.S. 660 (1983) at 670.

9. Bearden vs. Georgia, 461 U.S. 660 (1983) at 672.

10. Ibid.

11. Shapiro, Joseph. "Supreme Court Ruling Not Enough To Prevent Debtors Prisons." NPR. May 21, 2014. Accessed January 20, 2018. https://www.npr .org/2014/05/21/313118629/supreme-court-ruling-not-enough-to-prevent -debtors-prisons

12. Mount, Steve. "Amendment 14—Citizenship Rights." USConstitution.net. November 30, 2011. Accessed January 20, 2018. https://www.usconstitution .net/xconst_Am14.html

13. Head, Tom. "The Fifth Amendment: Text, Origins, and Meaning." *ThoughtCo.* January 3, 2018.Accessed January 20, 2018.https://www .thoughtco.com/the-fifth-amendment-721516.

14. *In re Connelly*, 59 B.R. 421 at 431 (Bankr. N.D. Ill. 1986).

15. Craig Gaumer & Charles Nail, "Truth or Consequences: The Dilemma of Asserting the Fifth Amendment Privilege Against Self-Incrimination in Bankruptcy Proceedings," 76 *Neb. L. Rev.* 497 (1997).

16. Ibid.

17. *In re Morganroth*, 718 F.2d 161 at 167 (6th Cir. 1983).

18. *In re French*, 127 B.R. 434 at 440 (Bankr. D. Minn. 1991).

19. 2008 Emerging Issues 3181, *Fifth Amendment Privilege in Bankruptcy Proceedings.*

20. McLean, Nicholas. "Livelihood, Ability to Pay, and the Original Meaning of the Excessive Fines Clause." 40 HASTINGS CONST. L.Q. 833 at 835 (2013).

21. An Overview of the 8th Amendment. Laws.com. Accessed January 20, 2018. https://constitution.laws.com/8th-amendment.

22. Ibid.

23. United States v. Bajakajian, 524 U.S. 321 (1998).

24. United States v. Smith, 656 F.3d 821, 828–29 (8th Cir. 2011); United States v. 817 N.E. 29th Drive, 175 F.3d 1304, 1311 (11th Cir. 1999).

25. McLean, Nicholas. "Livelihood, Ability to Pay, and the Original Meaning of the Excessive Fines Clause." 40 HASTINGS CONST. L.Q. 833 at 835 (2013).

26. Ibid.

27. Ibid.

28. The Heritage Foundation. 2017. Accessed January 21, 2018. https://www .heritage.org/constitution/#!/articles/1/essays/41/bankruptcy-clause.

29. Ibid.

30. Ibid.

31. Ibid.

32. Ibid.

33. Gibson, Kate. "How You Could Go to Debtors' Prison in the US" Money-Watch. March 21. 2016. Accessed January 21, 2018. https://www.cbsnews .com/news/how-you-could-go-to-debtors-prison-in-the-u-s/.

Chapter 3

1. Issa, Erin. "2017 American Household Credit Card Debt Study." Nerd Wallet. Accessed January 24, 2018. https://www.nerdwallet.com/blog/average-credit -card-debt-household/.

2. Jefferson, Gisele. "Become a Saver—Get Out of Debt First." *Journal-Advocate*. March 2, 2017. Accessed January 24, 2018. www.journal-advocate .com/sterling-community/ci_30829058/become-saver-get-out-debt-first.

3. Baillieul, Robert. "Household Debt Reaches Another Scary Record: Study." Income Investors. December 20, 2016. Accessed January 28, 2018. https:// www.incomeinvestors.com/household-debt-reaches-another-scary-record -study/11009/.

4. Johnson, Cody. "What's the Average American Household's Credit Card Debt?" Lexington Law. July 13, 2017. Accessed January 28, 2018. https:// www.lexingtonlaw.com/blog/credit/whats-the-average-american-households -credit-card-debt.html.

5. Issa, Erin. "2017 American Household Credit Card Debt Study." Nerd Wallet. Accessed January 28, 2018. https://www.nerdwallet.com/blog/average -credit-card-debt-household/.

6. Black, Simon. "Credit Suisse: with just $10, you're wealthier than 25% of Americans." SovereignMan. October 20, 2015. Accessed January 28, 2016. https://www.sovereignman.com/trends/credit-suisse-with-just-10-youre -wealthier-than-25-of-americans-18072/.

7. Ibid.

8. Pitts, Leonard. "Another View: Solving Middle-Class Debt Problems." *Daily Chronicle*. May 12, 2015. Accessed January 28, 2018. http://www.daily -chronicle.com/2015/05/13/another-view-solving-middle-class-debt-problem /aunvi44/.

9. Investopedia. "The Great Recession." Accessed January 29, 2018. https:// www.investopedia.com/terms/g/great-recession.asp.

10. Nutting, Rex. "Middle Class is Drowning in Debt, Hobbling the Economy." MarketWatch. June 27, 2014. Accessed January 29, 2018. https://www .marketwatch.com/story/middle-class-is-drowning-in-debt-hobbling-the -economy-2014-06-27.

11. Weil, Dan. "Middle-Class Debt Buildup Spells Doom for Economy." Newsmax. June 24, 2014. Accessed January 29, 2018. https://www.newsmax.com/Finance/Economy/middle-class-debt-economy/2014/06/30/id/579951/.

12. Mian, Atif and Sufi, Amir. "How they (and you) Caused the Great Depression, and how we can prevent it from happening again." *House of Debt.* May 30, 2014. Accessed January 29, 2018. http://www.press.uchicago.edu/ucp/books/book/chicago/H/bo20832545.html.

13. Nutting, Rex. "Middle Class is Drowning in Debt, Hobbling the Economy." MarketWatch, June 27, 2014. Accessed January 29, 2018. https://www.marketwatch.com/story/middle-class-is-drowning-in-debt-hobbling-the-economy-2014-06-27.

14. Ibid.

15. Ibid.

16. Treanor, Jill. "Half of world's wealth now in hands of 1% of population." *The Guardian.* October 13, 2015. Accessed January 29, 2018. https://www.theguardian.com/money/2015/oct/13/half-world-wealth-in-hands-population-inequality-report.

17. Nasser, Alan "The Myth of the Middle Class." *CounterPunch.* August 28, 2015. Accessed January 29, 2018. https://www.counterpunch.org/2015/08/28/the-myth-of-the-middle-class-have-most-americans-always-been-poor/.

18. Snyder, Michael. "Goodbye Middle Class: 51 Percent of all American Workers Make Less than 30,000 Dollars a Year." The American Dream. October 20, 2015. Accessed January 29, 2018. http://endoftheamericandream.com/archives/goodbye-middle-class-51-percent-of-all-american-workers-make-less-than-30000-dollars-a-year.

19. Ibid.

20. Ibid.

21. Ibid.

22. Heyes, J.D. "Middle Class Collapses in America as 35% of Households Face Debt Collectors." Natural News. August 10, 2014. Accessed January 29, 2018. https://www.naturalnews.com/046399_middle_class_debt_collectors_economic_collapse.html.

23. Mason, John. "How Fast Can the US Economy Grow With So Many Delinquent Loans?" The Street. July 31, 2018. Accessed January 29, 2018. https://

www.thestreet.com/story/12827261/1/how-can-fast-can-the-us-economy
-grow-with-so-many-delinquent-loans.html.

24. Geewax, Marilyn. "Chances Are Pretty Good That's A Bill Collector Call-
    ing." NPR. July 29, 2014. Accessed January 29, 2018. https://www.npr.org
    /sections/thetwo-way/2014/07/29/336322389/chances-are-pretty-good-that-s
    -a-bill-collector-calling.

25. Boak, Josh. "35 Percent of Americans Facing Debt Collectors." NBC. July 29,
    2014. Accessed January 29, 2018. https://www.nbcwashington.com/news
    /national-international/35-percent-of-Americans-Facing-Debt-Collectors
    -Study-269032031.html.

26. Nicholls, Elizabeth. "The History of Debt Collection." *The Advocate*. July
    2015. Accessed January 29, 2018. https://debtadvocate.co.uk/the-history-of
    -debt-collection/.

27. Boak, Josh. "35 Percent of Americans Facing Debt Collectors." *Wichita Eagle*.
    July 29, 2014. Accessed January 29, 2018. http://www.kansas.com/news
    /business/article1153336.html.

28. Ibid.

29. Ibid.

30. Heyes, J.D. "Middle Class Collapses in America as 35% of Households Face
    Debt Collectors." Natural News. August 10, 2014. Accessed January 29,
    2018. https://www.naturalnews.com/046399_middle_class_debt_collectors
    _economic_collapse.html.

31. 2015 Annual Report. GreenPath. http://www.greenpath.com/docs/GP_AR
    _2015.pdf.

32. Heyes, J.D. "Middle Class Collapses in America as 35% of Households Face
    Debt Collectors." Natural News. August 10, 2014. Accessed January 29,
    2018. https://www.naturalnews.com/046399_middle_class_debt_collectors
    _economic_collapse.html.

Chapter 4

1. Brennan Center for Justice. December 9, 2016. Accessed January 30, 2018.
   https://www.brennancenter.org/press-release/new-report-39-percent-prisoners
   -are-unnecessarily-behind-bars.

2. Ladeji, Tomi. "You Could be Committing a Crime and Not Even Know it." Real Clear Policy. March 27, 2017. Accessed January 30, 2018. https://www .realclearpolicy.com/articles/2017/03/27/you_could_be_committing_a_crime _and_not_even_know_it_110200.html.

3. Ibid.

4. Arkin, Paul. "The Extend of America's Overcriminalization Problem." *The Heritage Foundation*. May 9, 2014. Accessed January 30, 2018. https://www .heritage.org/report/the-extent-americas-overcriminalization-problem.

5. Ibid.

6. Ibid.

7. Ibid.

8. Ladeji, Tomi. "You Could be Committing a Crime and Not Even Know it." Real Clear Policy. March 27, 2017. Accessed January 30, 2018. https://www .realclearpolicy.com/articles/2017/03/27/you_could_be_committing_a_crime _and_not_even_know_it_110200.html.

9. Eldridge, Lance. "All Law Enforcement is Local." PoliceOne Network. August 10, 2011. Accessed January 30, 2018. https://www.policeone.com /federal-law-enforcement/articles/4147493-Overcriminalization-and-police -officer-safety/.

10. Ladeji, Tomi. "You Could be Committing a Crime and Not Even Know it." Real Clear Policy. March 27, 2017. Accessed January 30, 2018. https://www .realclearpolicy.com/articles/2017/03/27/you_could_be_committing_a_crime _and_not_even_know_it_110200.html.

11. Dieterle, C. Jarrett. "Gorsuch v. Overcriminalization." R Street. February 24, 2017. Accessed January 30, 2018. https://www.rstreet.org/op-ed/gorsuch-v -overcriminalization/.

12. Ibid.

13. Ibid.

14. Sussman, Barry. "How Many Convicted Felons are there in the U.S? It's a Mystery." Open News. May 7, 2014. Accessed February 2, 2018. https://www .opednews.com/articles/How-Many-Convicted-Felons-by-Barry-Sussman -Crime_Criminal_Disenfranchisement_Felons-140507-368.html.

15. Ibid.

16. Eldridge, Lance. "All Law Enforcement is Local." PoliceOne Network. August 10, 2011. Accessed January 30, 2018. https://www.policeone.com

/federal-law-enforcement/articles/4147493-Overcriminalization-and-police
-officer-safety/.

17. Zakaria, Fareed. "Incarceration Nation: The War on Drugs has Succeeded
only in Putting Millions of Americans in Jail." *Time Magazine.* April 2, 2012.
Accessed February 2, 2018. http://content.time.com/time/magazine/article
/0,9171,2109777,00.html.

18. Correa, Tom. "Making American a Nation of Felons." The American Cow-
boy Chronicles. April 8, 2013. Accessed February 2, 2018. http://www
.americancowboychronicles.com/2013/04/making-america-nation-of-felons
_8.html.

19. Eldridge, Lance. "All Law Enforcement is Local." PoliceOne Network.
August 10, 2011. Accessed January 30, 2018. https://www.policeone.com
/federal-law-enforcement/articles/4147493-Overcriminalization-and-police
-officer-safety/.

20. Ibid.

21. Ibid.

22. Correa, Tom. "Making American a Nation of Felons." The American Cow-
boy Chronicles. April 8, 2013. Accessed February 2, 2018. http://www
.americancowboychronicles.com/2013/04/making-america-nation-of-felons
_8.html.

23. Sussman, Barry. "How Many Convicted Felons are there in the U.S? It's a
Mystery." Open News. May 7, 2014. Accessed February 2, 2018. https://www
.opednews.com/articles/How-Many-Convicted-Felons-by-Barry-Sussman
-Crime_Criminal_Disenfranchisement_Felons-140507-368.html.

24. Eldridge, Lance. "All Law Enforcement is Local." PoliceOne Network.
August 10, 2011. Accessed January 30, 2018. https://www.policeone.com
/federal-law-enforcement/articles/4147493-Overcriminalization-and-police
-officer-safety/.

25. SPLC. "Alabama Town Agrees in Settlement to Stop Operating Debtors'
Prison." Southern Poverty Law Center. March 14, 2017. Accessed February 2,
2018. https://www.splcenter.org/news/2017/03/14/alabama-town-agrees
-settlement-stop-operating-debtors'-prison.

26. Ibid.

27. Ibid.

28. Rhodes, Robert. "Unlawful Recreational Fishing | A Defense Lawyer's Viewpoint | Criminal Problems in the State of Washington." Rhodes Legal Group. Accessed February 3, 2018. https://rhodeslegalgroup.com/criminal-law /recreational-fishing/.

29. Ibid.

30. Ibid.

31. Ellis, Blake. "Shockingly Small 'Crimes,' that can Land you in Jail." CNN Money. April 10, 2015. Accessed February 3, 2018. http://money.cnn.com /2015/04/09/pf/arrest-warrant-jail/index.html.

32. Lewis, Dan. "A Fishy Sentence." *Now I Know*. Simon & Schuster. June 20, 2016. Accessed February 3, 2018. http://nowiknow.com/a-fishy-sentence/.

33. ACLU. "Jailing People Because They Are Too Poor to Pay Legal Fees Is Unconstitutional." August 4, 2011. Accessed February 3, 2018. https://www .aclu.org/news/aclu-challenges-debtors-prisons-across-michigan.

34. Ibid.

Chapter 5

1. Davidson, Adam. "Is College Tuition Really Too High?" *New York Times*. September 28, 2015. Accessed February 3, 2018. https://www.nytimes .com/2015/09/13/magazine/is-college-tuition-too-high.html.

2. Kantrowitz, Mark "Why the Student Loan Crisis Is Even Worse Than People Think." *Time*. January 11, 2016. Accessed February 3. 2018. http://time.com /money/4168510/why-student-loan-crisis-is-worse-than-people-think/.

3. Ibid.

4. Reuters. "What Happens if you Lie on your FAFSA?" July 14, 2015. Fox Business. Accessed February 3, 2018. http://www.foxbusiness.com/features/2015 /07/14/what-happens-if-lie-on-your-fafsa.html.

5. Wallin, Paul. "Consequences of Filing a Fraudulent Claim for Student Financial Aid." Wallin & Klarich Law. Accessed February 3, 2018. https://www .wklaw.com/fraudulent-claim-for-student-financial-aid/.

6. Ibid.

7. Ibid.

8. Ibid.

9. Reuters. "What Happens if you Lie on your FAFSA?" July 14, 2015. Fox Business. Accessed February 3, 2018. http://www.foxbusiness.com/features/2015/07/14/what-happens-if-lie-on-your-fafsa.html.

10. Ibid.

11. Ibid.

12. Kantrowitz, Mark "Why the Student Loan Crisis Is Even Worse Than People Think." *Time*. January 11, 2016. Accessed February 3. 2018. http://time.com/money/4168510/why-student-loan-crisis-is-worse-than-people-think/.

13. Friedman, Zack. "Student Loan Debt In 2017: A $1.3 Trillion Crisis." *Forbes*. February 23, 2017. Accessed February 4, 2018. https://www.forbes.com/forbes/welcome/?toURL=https://www.forbes.com/sites/zackfriedman/2017/02/21/student-loan-debt-statistics-2017/&refURL=https://www.bing.com/&referrer=https://www.bing.com/.

14. Kantrowitz, Mark. "Why the Student Loan Crisis Is Even Worse Than People Think." *Time*. January 11, 2016. Accessed February 3, 2018. http://time.com/money/4168510/why-student-loan-crisis-is-worse-than-people-think/.

15. Ibid.

16. Ibid.

17. Jackson, Abby. "These are the 4 horrible things that can happen if you default on your student loans." Business Insider. February 27, 2016. Accessed February 4, 2018. http://www.businessinsider.com/heres-what-happens-when-you-default-on-student-loans-2016-2.

18. CNN. "Man Arrested by US Marshals for Unpaid $1,500 Student Loan." February 16, 2016. Accessed February 4, 2018. http://fox40.com/2016/02/16/man-arrested-by-u-s-marshals-for-unpaid-1500-student-loan/.

19. Jackson, Abby. "These are the 4 horrible things that can happen if you default on your student loans." Business Insider. February 27, 2016. Accessed February 4, 2018. http://www.businessinsider.com/heres-what-happens-when-you-default-on-student-loans-2016-2.

20. CNN. "Man Arrested by US Marshals for Unpaid $1,500 Student Loan." February 16, 2016. Accessed February 4, 2018. http://fox40.com/2016/02/16/man-arrested-by-u-s-marshals-for-unpaid-1500-student-loan/.

21. Ibid.

22. Jackson, Abby. "These are the 4 horrible things that can happen if you default on your student loans." Business Insider. February 27, 2016. Accessed

February 4, 2018. http://www.businessinsider.com/heres-what-happens
-when-you-default-on-student-loans-2016-2.

23. Parks, Michael. "Operation Anaconda Squeeze Leads to Arrests of Debtors in
Minnesota." *Student Life*. February 13, 2003. Accessed February 4, 2018.
http://www.studlife.com/archives/News/2003/02/21
/OperationAnacondaSqueezeleadstoarrestsofdebtorsinMinnesota/.

24. Ibid.

25. Argento, Michelle. "Can You be Arrested For Failing to Pay your Student
Debt?" Student Loan Hero. February 19, 2016. Accessed February 5, 2018.
https://studentloanhero.com/featured/can-you-be-arrested-for-not-paying
-student-loans/.

26. Ibid.

27. Jackson, Abby. "These are the 4 horrible things that can happen if you
default on your student loans." Business Insider. February 27, 2016. Accessed
February 4, 2018. http://www.businessinsider.com/heres-what-happens-when
-you-default-on-student-loans-2016-2.

28. Ibid.

29. Ibid.

30. Ibid.

31. Ibid.

32. Ibid.

Chapter 6

1. Ellis, Blake. "Shockingly small 'crimes' that can land you in jail." CNN
Money. April 10, 2015. Accessed February 7, 2018. http://money.cnn.com
/2015/04/09/pf/arrest-warrant-jail/index.html.

2. Ibid.

3. Ibid.

4. Snead, Jason. "Students Will No Longer Face Jail Time for Missing School in
Texas." The Daily Signal. June 30, 2015. Accessed February 11, 2018. http://
dailysignal.com/2015/06/30/students-will-no-longer-face-jail-time-for-missing
-school-in-texas/.

5. Ibid.

6. Ibid.

7. Ibid.

8. Ibid.

9. Gregorian, Dareh. "Littering, public urination and other minor offenses in Manhattan will lead to summons and not arrest." *Daily News*. March 1, 2016. Accessed February 12, 2 018. http://www.nydailynews.com/new-york/nyc-crime/minor-offenses-manhattan-no-longer-result-arrests-article-1.2549474.

10. Ibid.

11. Ibid.

12. Durkin, Erin. "NYC council speaker to propose purging old warrants for small crimes like public drinking, park violations." *Daily News*. February 10, 2016. Accessed February 12, 2018. http://www.nydailynews.com/news/politics/nyc-pol-eyes-plan-purge-warrants-small-crimes-article-1.2527430.

13. Gregorian, Dareh. "Littering, public urination and other minor offenses in Manhattan will lead to summons and not arrest." *Daily News*. March 1, 2016. Accessed February 12, 2 018. http://www.nydailynews.com/new-york/nyc-crime/minor-offenses-manhattan-no-longer-result-arrests-article-1.2549474.

14. Ellis, Blake. "The Secret World of Government Debt Collection." February 17, 2015. CNN Money. Accessed February 12, 2018. http://money.cnn.com/interactive/pf/debt-collector/government-agencies/index.html.

15. Ibid.

16. Ibid.

17. Ellis, Blake. "The Secret World of Government Debt Collection." February 17, 2015. CNN Money. Accessed February 12, 2018. http://money.cnn.com/interactive/pf/debt-collector/nightmares/index.html.

18. Ibid.

19. Ellis, Blake. "The Secret World of Government Debt Collection." February 17, 2015. CNN Money. Accessed February 12, 2018. http://money.cnn.com/interactive/pf/debt-collector/government-agencies/index.html.

20. Ibid.

21. Ibid.

22. Ibid.

23. Ibid.

24. Ibid.

25. Lehman, Don. "Tax fraud charges against Queensbury businessman dropped." *The Pop Star*. April 5, 2012. Accessed February 13, 2018. http://poststar.com/news/local/tax-fraud-charges-against-queensbury-businessman-dropped/article_392884c4-7f66-11e1-8c0d-001a4bcf887a.html.

26. Ibid.

27. Ibid.

28. Rector-Gable, Mary. "Tax Season Alert: Can a Salon Get In Trouble for Stylists Not Reporting Tips?" Behind the Chair.com. January 22, 2015. Accessed February 13, 2018Behind the Chair. https://behindthechair.com/articles/tax-season-alert-can-a-salon-get-in-trouble-for-stylists-not-reporting-tips/.

29. Ibid.

30. Turbo Tax. "How to Claim Tips on Your Tax Return." Updated for year 2017. Accessed February 14, 2018. https://turbotax.intuit.com/tax-tips/jobs-and-career/how-to-claim-tips-on-your-tax-return/L2xnHeQvl.

31. Ibid.

32. LawFirms.com. "Tax Frauds and Crimes." Accessed February 14, 2018.

33. http://www.lawfirms.com/resources/tax/tax-fraud-and-tax-evasion/tax-fraud-and-crimes.htm.

34. Ibid.

35. Ibid.

36. Ibid.

37. Ibid.

Chapter 7

1. Ellis, Blake. "Shockingly Small 'Crimes' That Can Land You In Jail." CNN Money. April 10, 2015. Accessed February 7, 2018. http://money.cnn.com/2015/04/09/pf/arrest-warrant-jail/index.html.

2. Ibid.

3. Statista. "The Number of Licensed Drivers in the US from 1990–2016." Accessed February 16, 2018. https://www.statista.com/statistics/191653/number-of-licensed-drivers-in-the-us-since-1988/.

4. Statistic Brain. "Driving Citation Statistics." July 8, 2014. Accessed February 16, 2018. https://www.statisticbrain.com/driving-citation-statistics/.

5. The Newspaper.com. "Nashville, Tennessee Mayor Orders 33 Percent Ticket Increase." May 29, 2006. Accessed February 16, 2018. https://www.thenewspaper.com/news/11/1154.asp.

6. Maciag, Mike. "Skyrocketing Court Fines Are Major Revenue Generator for Ferguson." August 22, 2014. Accessed February 16, 2018. http://www.governing.com/topics/public-justice-safety/gov-ferguson-missouri-court-fines-budget.html.

7. Clark, Maggie. "Red-light cameras generate revenue, controversy." *USA Today*. October 15, 2013. Accessed February 16, 2018. https://www.usatoday.com/story/news/nation/2013/10/15/stateline-red-light-cameras/2986577/.

8. Safe Motorist.Com. "Do Traffic Quotas Really Exist?" American Safety Council. June 25, 2013. Accessed February 16, 2018. http://www.safemotorist.com/articles/traffic_ticket_quotas.aspx.

9. Sarkissian, Arek. "Interim Waldo Police Chief Also Suspended Over Ticket Quota." *Gainesville Sun*. August 28, 2014. Accessed February 16, 2018. http://www.gainesville.com/article/LK/20140828/News/604154734/GS/.

10. Terruso, Julia. "East Orange police quarrel over claims of ticketing quotas." *The Star-Ledger*. Accessed March 25, 2013. February 16, 2018. http://www.nj.com/essex/index.ssf/2013/03/east_orange_police_tickets_quo.html.

11. Autoblog. Police Across "USA Charged With Traffic Ticket Quotas To Meet Budgets." September 6, 2013. Accessed February 16, 2018. https://www.autoblog.com/2013/09/06/police-usa-traffic-ticket-quotas-budgets/.

12. Ibid.

13. ACLU. "The Prison Crisis." January 20, 2015. Accessed January 16, 2018. https://www.aclu.org/prison-crisis.

14. Berrien, Hank. "DOJ: Don't Send People To Jail If They Don't Pay Fines." The Daily Wire. March 14, 2016. Accessed February 16, 2018. https://www.dailywire.com/news/4109/doj-dont-send-people-jail-if-they-dont-pay-fines-hank-berrien.

15. Scott, Kimberly. "Legally Speaking: The Cops are at the Door." *Primer*. January 5, 2016. Accessed February 16, 2018. https://www.primermagazine.com/2013/learn/legally-speaking-police-are-at-the-door.

16. Seville, Lisa. "Sentenced to Debt: Some tossed in Prison Over Unpaid Fines." NBC In Plain Sight. May 27, 2013. Accessed February 16, 2018. https://www

.nbcnews.com/feature/in-plain-sight/sentenced-debt-some-tossed-prison-over -unpaid-fines-v18380470.

17. Bronner, Ethan. "Poor Land in Jail as Companies Add Huge Fees for Probation." *New York Times*. July 2, 2012. Accessed February 16, 2018. http:// www.nytimes.com/2012/07/03/us/probation-fees-multiply-as-companies -profit.html.

18. Kincade, Brian. "The Economics of the American Prison System." Smart-Asset. February 3, 2017. Accessed February 16, 2018. https://smartasset.com /mortgage/the-economics-of-the-american-prison-system.

19. Huling, Tracy. "Building a Prison Economy in Rural America." *The New Press*. May 5, 2012. Accessed February 16, 2018. https://www.prisonpolicy .org/scans/building.html.

20. Kincade, Brian. "The Economics of the American Prison System." Smart-Asset. February 3, 2017. Accessed February 16, 2018. https://smartasset.com /mortgage/the-economics-of-the-american-prison-system.

21. Ibid.

22. Ibid.

23. Ibid.

24. Picchi, Aimee. "In Modern-Day Debtors' Prisons, Courts Team with Private Sector." CBS MoneyWatch. March 25, 2015. Accessed February 16, 2018. https://www.cbsnews.com/news/the-rise-of-americas-debtor-prisons/.

25. Slavo, Mac. "Short on Cash: Poor Americans Ending Up in Modern-Day Debtors' Prison Over Traffic Fines." SHTFplan.com. April 1, 2015. Accessed February 16, 2018. http://www.shtfplan.com/headline-news/short-on-cash -poor-americans-ending-up-in-modern-day-debtors-prison-over-traffic-fines _04012015.

26. Picchi, Aimee. "In Modern-Day Debtors' Prisons, Courts Team with Private Sector." CBS MoneyWatch. March 25, 2015. Accessed February 16, 2018. https://www.cbsnews.com/news/the-rise-of-americas-debtor-prisons/.

27. Ibid.

28. Ibid.

29. Ibid.

30. Sherter, Alain. "As Economy Flails, Debtors' Prisons Thrive." CBS Money-Watch. April 5, 2013. Accessed February 16, 2018. https://www.cbsnews .com/news/as-economy-flails-debtors-prisons-thrive/.

31. Beitsch, Rebecca. "Paying Court Debt By Working it Off." *HuffPost*. April 4, 2017. Accessed February 17, 2018. https://www.huffingtonpost.com/entry/paying-court-debt-by-working-it-off_us_58e3a725e4b09dbd42f3da62.

32. Ibid.

33. Ibid.

34. Ibid.

35. Ibid.

Chapter 8

1. National Vital Statistics System. "National Marriage and Divorce Trends, 2000–2014." CDC. November 23, 2015. Accessed February 17, 2018. https://www.cdc.gov/nchs/nvss/marriage_divorce_tables.htm.

2. Robles, Frances. "Skip Child Support. Go to Jail. Lose Job. Repeat." *New York Times*. April 19, 2015. Accessed February 17, 2018. https://www.nytimes.com/2015/04/20/us/skip-child-support-go-to-jail-lose-job-repeat.html.

3. Meyer, Cathy. "What Your Divorce Attorney Won't Tell You About Marital Debt." *HuffPost*. March 2, 2014. Accessed February 17, 2018. https://www.huffingtonpost.com/2014/03/02/marital-debt_n_4861960.html.

4. Ibid.

5. Ibid.

6. Ibid.

7. Ibid.

8. Achen, Tracy. "When Divorce and Bankruptcy Collide." WomansDivorce.com. Accessed February 17, 2018. https://www.womansdivorce.com/divorce-and-bankruptcy.html.

9. Ibid.

10. Ibid.

11. Ibid.

12. Finley, Gordon. "Deadbeat Fathers and Return of Imprisonment for Deadbeat Fathers and Return of Imprisonment for Debt." *Wall Street Journal*. March 17, 2015. Accessed February 17, 2018. https://www.wsj.com/article_email/deadbeat-fathers-and-return-of-imprisonment-for-debt-letters-to-the-editor-1426536258-lMyQjAxMTI1NzEyNjgxNzYwWj.

13. Wolf, Jennifer. "Deadbeat Dad Stereotypes & the Issue of Unpaid Child Support." The Spruce. October 2, 2017. Accessed February 17, 2018. https://www.thespruce.com/deadbeat-parents-and-help-for-affected-families-2997665.

14. Washington, Debrina. "Failure to Pay Child Support—6 Penalties for Parents who Fail to Pay Child Support." The Spruce. Accessed June 12, 2017. February 18, 2018. https://www.thespruce.com/failure-to-pay-child-support-penalties-2997972.

15. Ibid.

16. Ibid.

17. Ibid.

18. Walters, Jonathan. "Is Jailing Deadbeat Dads Effective?" Governing.com. July 16, 2013. Accessed February 17, 2018. http://www.governing.com/topics/health-human-services/col-jailing-deadbeat-dads-effective-child-support-payments.html.

19. Ibid.

20. Ibid.

21. Ibid.

22. Cammet, Ann. "When Deadbeat Dads Are Jailed." *New York Times*. April 28, 2015. Accessed February 18, 2018. https://www.nytimes.com/2015/04/28/opinion/when-deadbeat-dads-are-jailed.html.

23. Ibid.

24. Ibid.

25. Robinson, Walter. "Law and Empathy at Issue in Jailing of a Debtor." *Boston Globe*. July 2, 2014. Accessed February 18, 2018. http://www.bostonglobe.com/metro/2014/07/01/elderly-small-court-debtor-sent-jail/R2bgRLxbc5eTmSTGYW3k9L/story.html.

26. Ibid.

27. Ibid.

28. Ibid.

29. Ibid.

30. Ibid.

Chapter 9

1. ACLU. "In For A Penny: The Rise of America's New Debtors' Prison." American Civil Liberties Union. October 2010. Accessed January 5, 2018. https://www.aclu.org/report/penny-rise-americas-new-debtors-prisons.

2. Ibid.

3. Ibid.

4. Ibid.

5. Ibid.

6. Ibid.

7. Ibid.

8. Ibid.

9. Ibid.

10. 42 U.S.C. § 608(a)(9)(A); 7 U.S.C. § 2015(k)(1); 42 U.S.C. § 1437d(1)(9); 42 U.S.C. § 1382(e)(4)(A)(ii).

11. Patel, Roopal. "Criminal Justice for Debt: A Toolkit for Action." Brennan Center for Justice. March 2012. Accessed January 7, 2018. https://www.brennancenter.org/sites/default/files/legacy/publications/Criminal%20Justice%20Debt%20Background%20for%20web.pdf.

12. Ibid.

13. Ibid.

14. R.I.G.L. Section 12-6-7.1.

15. R.I.G.L. §12-21-20(d).

16. R.I.G.L. §12-21-20(c) and §12-6-7.1(b).

17. R.I.G.L. §12-20-10(b).

18. R.I.G.L. §11-25-15.

19. ACLU. "A Pound of Flesh: The Criminalization of Private Debt." American Civil Liberties Union. February 21, 2018. Accessed February 26, 2018. https://www.aclu.org/report/pound-flesh-criminalization-private-debt.

Chapter 10

1. Austin, John. "Debtors Prisons For Drivers Gets New Scrutiny." CNHI News. January 26, 2017. Accessed February 19, 2018. http://www.cnhinews.com/cnhi/article_0e858154-e41f-11e6-a988-5f924524ee60.html.

2. Sherter, Alain. "As Economy Flails, Debtors' Prisons Thrive." CBS Money-Watch. April 5, 2013. Accessed February 16, 2018. https://www.cbsnews.com/news/as-economy-flails-debtors-prisons-thrive/.

3. Seville, Lisa. "Sentenced to Debt: Some tossed in Prison Over Unpaid Fines." NBC In Plain Sight. May 27, 2013. Accessed February 16, 2018. https://www.nbcnews.com/feature/in-plain-sight/sentenced-debt-some-tossed-prison-over-unpaid-fines-v18380470.

4. Ibid.

5. Ibid.

6. Ibid.

7. Ibid

8. Kane, Alex. "Miss a Traffic Ticket, Go to Jail; The Return of Debtor Prison." *AlterNet.* February 3, 2013. Accessed February 19, 2018. https://www.alternet.org/miss-traffic-ticket-go-jail-return-debtor-prison-hard-times-usa.

9. Whitehead, John. "America's Growing Police State." *The Patriots: News From Citizen Advocates.* September 6, 2012. Accessed February 19, 2018. http://www.newpatriotsblog.com/news/americas-growing-police-state-/.

10. Will, George. "Leviathan on a Fishing Expedition." *Human Events.* July 28, 2012. Accessed February 19, 2018. http://humanevents.com/2012/07/28/george-will-leviathan-on-a-fishing-expedition/.

11. Ibid.

12. WEAC. "Prison spending is dramatically outpacing education spending, US Department of Education Says." *Wisconsin Education Association Council.* July 18, 2016. Accessed February 19, 2018. http://weac.org/2016/07/18/prison-spending-dramatically-outpacing-education-spending-u-s-department-education-says/.

13. Brown, Emma. "Since 1980, spending on prisons has grown three times as much as spending on public education." *Washington Post.* July 2, 2016. Accessed February 19, 2018. https://www.washingtonpost.com/news/education/wp/2016/07/07/since-1980-spending-on-prisons-has-grown-three-times-faster-than-spending-on-public-education/?utm_term=.d949a6ab1a52.

14. Ibid.

15. Ibid.

16. Ibid.

17. AP. "Justices: Colorado Policy on Court Fees Unconstitutional." *US News & World Report*. April 19, 2017. Accessed February 19, 2018. https://www .usnews.com/news/politics/articles/2017-04-19/justices-colorado-policy-on -court-fees-unconstitutional.

18. Ibid.

19. ACLU. "Ending Modern-Day Debtors' Prisons." Accessed February 19, 2018. https://www.aclu.org/issues/criminal-law-reform/sentencing/ending-modern -day-debtors-prisons.

20. Ibid.

Chapter 11

1. Carney, John. "The US Government Cannot Ever Run Out of Money." *The Atlantic*. July 22, 2011. Accessed February 19, 2008. https://www.theatlantic .com/business/archive/2011/07/the-us-government-cannot-ever-run-out-of -money/242622/.

2. Ibid.

3. Ibid.

4. Ibid.

5. Fay, Bill. "Timeline of US Federal Debt Since Independence Day 1776." Debt.org. July 4, 2013. Accessed February 20, 2018. https://www.debt.org /blog/united-states-federal-debt-timeline/.

6. Ibid.

7. Ibid.

8. Ibid.

9. Amadeo, Kimberly. "Who Owns the US National Debt?" The Balance. January 24, 2018. Accessed February 20, 2018. https://www.thebalance.com/who -owns-the-u-s-national-debt-3306124.

10. Tucker, Will. "America The Trumped." Southern Poverty Law Center. January 19, 2018. Accessed February 19, 2018. https://www.splcenter.org /20180119/america-trumped-10-ways-administration-attacked-civil-rights -year-one.

11. Tesfaye, Sophie. "The Return of Debtors' Prisons: Jeff Sessions' War on the Poor." Truthout. December 31, 2017. Accessed February 19, 2018. http://

www.truth-out.org/news/item/43084-a-return-to-debtors-prisons-jeff-sessions
-war-on-the-poor.

12. US Department of Justice. "Organization, Mission and Functions Manual:
Office of Attorney General." Accessed February 20, 2018. https://www
.justice.gov/jmd/organization-mission-and-functions-manual-attorney
-general.

13. US Department of Justice—Office of Public Affairs. "Fact Sheet on White
House and Justice Department Convening—A Cycle of Incarceration: Prison,
Debt and Bail Practices." December 3, 2015. Accessed February 20, 2018.
https://www.justice.gov/opa/pr/fact-sheet-white-house-and-justice-department
-convening-cycle-incarceration-prison-debt-and.

14. Ibid.

15. Zapotosky, Matt. "Justice Department warns local courts about unlawful
fines and fees." *Washington Post*. March 14, 2016. Accessed February 20,
2018. https://www.washingtonpost.com/world/national-security/justice
-department-warns-local-courts-about-unlawful-fines-and-fees/2016/03/13
/c475df18-e939-11e5-a6f3-21ccdbc5f74e_story.html?utm_term
=.caac13e5483e.

16. Ibid.

17. Ibid.

18. Tucker, Will. "America The Trumped." Southern Poverty Law Center. January 19, 2018. Accessed February 19, 2018. https://www.splcenter.org
/20180119/america-trumped-10-ways-administration-attacked-civil-rights
-year-one.

19. Tesfaye, Sophie. "The Return of Debtors' Prisons: Jeff Sessions' War on the
Poor." Truthout. December 31, 2017. Accessed February 19, 2018. http://
www.truth-out.org/news/item/43084-a-return-to-debtors-prisons-jeff-sessions
-war-on-the-poor.

20. Blevins, Rachel. "War On the Poor." Activist Post. December 30, 2017.
Accessed February 19, 2018. https://www.activistpost.com/2017/12/jeff
-sessions-rescinds-legal-doc-allow-debtors-prisons.html.

21. Ibid.

22. Tesfaye, Sophie. "The Return of Debtors' Prisons: Jeff Sessions' War on the
Poor." Truthout. December 31, 2017. Accessed February 19, 2018. http://

www.truth-out.org/news/item/43084-a-return-to-debtors-prisons-jeff-sessions
-war-on-the-poor.

23. Ibid.